Python Recipes Handbook

A Problem-Solution Approach

Joey Bernard

Apress®

Python Recipes Handbook: A Problem-Solution Approach

Joey Bernard
Fredericton, New Brunswick, Canada

ISBN-13 (pbk): 978-1-4842-0242-5
DOI 10.1007/978-1-4842-0241-8

ISBN-13 (electronic): 978-1-4842-0241-8

Library of Congress Control Number: 2016958438

Managing Director: Welmoed Spahr
Lead Editor: Steve Anglin
Technical Reviewer: Michael Thomas
Editorial Board: Steve Anglin, Pramila Balan, Laura Berendson, Aaron Black, Louise Corrigan,
    Jonathan Gennick, Robert Hutchinson, Celestin Suresh John, Nikhil Karkal,
    James Markham, Susan McDermott, Matthew Moodie, Natalie Pao, Gwenan Spearing
Coordinating Editor: Mark Powers
Copy Editor: Mary Behr
Compositor: SPi Global
Indexer: SPi Global
Artist: SPi Global

Distributed to the book trade worldwide by Springer Science+Business Media New York, 233 Spring Street, 6th Floor, New York, NY 10013. Phone 1-800-SPRINGER, fax (201) 348-4505, e-mail orders-ny@springer-sbm.com, or visit www.springeronline.com. Apress Media, LLC is a California LLC and the sole member (owner) is Springer Science + Business Media Finance Inc (SSBM Finance Inc). SSBM Finance Inc is a Delaware corporation.

For information on translations, please e-mail rights@apress.com, or visit www.apress.com.

Apress and friends of ED books may be purchased in bulk for academic, corporate, or promotional use. eBook versions and licenses are also available for most titles. For more information, reference our Special Bulk Sales–eBook Licensing web page at www.apress.com/bulk-sales.

Any source code or other supplementary materials referenced by the author in this text are available to readers at www.apress.com. For detailed information about how to locate your book's source code, go to www.apress.com/source-code/. Readers can also access source code at SpringerLink in the Supplementary Material section for each chapter.

Printed on acid-free paper

This book is dedicated to my loving wife, patient enough to put up with my late nights of writing. It is also dedicated to my two boys, who were always willing to come tell Dad that he had to take a break from writing and spend time goofing off with them.

Contents at a Glance

Contents

About the Author

Joey Bernard has written several articles for *Linux Journal* and *Linux User and Developer*, and currently has a regular column in each magazine. In his day job with ACENET and Compute Canada, he helps university researchers with all of their computational work. This job lets him make use of both his physics degree and his computer science degree. A leader ensures that he doesn't spend all of his time indoors.

About the Technical Reviewer

Michael Thomas has worked in software development for more than 20 years as an individual contributor, team lead, program manager, and vice president of engineering. Michael has more than 10 years of experience working with mobile devices. His current focus is in the medical sector, using mobile devices to accelerate information transfer between patients and health care providers.

Acknowledgments

This book would not have seen the light of day without the unbelievable patience and consistent prodding of the Apress editorial team, specifically Mark Powers and Steve Anglin. Thank you both for putting up with the delays and helping me to keep on schedule.

I would also like to thank my wife, Laurel, and my boys, Evan and Sean, for their patience when Dad had to stay up late writing.

Introduction

Python is a very popular and powerful programming language. Its growth has been especially prevelant within the sciences. A cost of this power is that there is a steep learning curve when discovering everything that you can possibly do with Python. This is where this book can hopefully fill in some of that steep curve. I have attempted to expose the reader to many different areas where Python is used, along with recipes of how to actually use Python within each of these areas. The assumption is that you, the reader, have at least enough experience with Python to be able to read it comfortably and understand what a snippet of code is doing.

Chapter 1 covers the string classes and the tools available to do text processing. It also covers some of the caveats caused by how Python stores and handles string objects.

Chapter 2 covers how Python handles numbers, and how to handle dates and times. There are also tools for formatting dates and times, and ways to manipulate them.

Chapter 3 covers iterators and generators, and how they can be used to handle processing workflows that are best handled by iterating over some set of data elements.

Chapter 4 covers files, and how to handle input and output operations with the operating system of the machine where your Python code is running.

Chapter 5 introduces the package named pandas and how to use it to handle larger datasets. It also includes a set of tools for manipulating these datasets and doing processing and statistics on them.

Chapter 6 looks at how functions work in Python in more detail. It also covers how to manipulate them and change them dynamically.

Chapter 7 dives into classes and objects in more detail, looking at the details of how Python handles them. It also looks into how to manipulate them in unique ways.

Chapter 8 introduces metaprogramming and how this can be done in Python. It looks at ways to affect functions and classes, such as using decorators or metaclasses.

Chapter 9 covers how to interact with the Internet, using both standard protocols (like HTTP) and low-level raw sockets for sending and receiving data.

Chapter 10 looks at how modules and packages are created, and how you can bundle your own code into a form that is easily redistributable.

Chapter 11 introduces numpy, the key package used in scientific programming. It is the core dependency for many of the other scientific packages available within the Python community.

Chapter 12 looks at some of the available options when you are ready to parallelize your code to get better performance out of your programs.

Chapter 13 introduces some of the external utilities that are so popular that they have essentially become part of the Python environment.

Chapter 14 covers the basics of debugging your code, looking for performance issues. It also looks at the basics of the builtin debugger, pdb, to be able to step through your code within Python.

Chapter 15 looks at the true superpower of Python: the ability to easily use compiled C code and import it into your Python program for sections of code that need to perform extremely well. It also covers the basics of how to run Python code from within a C program, allowing you to reuse code already written for Python.

Chapter 16 introduces the basics of interacting with two of the most popular small form machines for DIY projects: the microcontroller Arduino and the single board computer (SBC) Raspberry Pi.

CHAPTER 1

Strings and Texts

Since the earliest days of computing, data used in computations was stored in basic text files. Anyone who has written shell scripts knows all too well that Unix systems and their utilities are built around the assumption that processing text will be much of the work of the program. Python is no different; it provides several programming elements to help with basic text processing tasks.

To begin, let's note how Python stores strings. Strings are immutable lists, so they cannot be changed. Any change to a string's contents requires making copies to new locations in memory. You must always keep this in mind when you try to optimize any text processing portions of your code.

1-1. Concatenating Strings

Problem

You want to build strings up from a number of smaller strings. This process is called *concatenation.*

Solution

The simplest way to build up a string is to use the + operator. In this case, the strings are put together and the complete new string is returned.

How It Works

Listing 1-1 shows an example.

Listing 1-1. Basic Concatenation

```
>>> new_str = "hello " + "world"
>>> print(new_str)
hello world
```

© Joey Bernard 2016
J. Bernard, *Python Recipes Handbook*, DOI 10.1007/978-1-4842-0241-8_1

This code returns the string "hello world". If you want a space between the two words, you need to explicitly add a space to one of the strings.

You can also create strings from multiple copies of a smaller string. This is done by using the * operator and essentially *multiplying* by the number of copies you want. See Listing 1-2 for an example.

Listing 1-2. Multiplicative Concatenation

```
>>> new_str = "Hello" * 3
>>> print(new_str)
HelloHelloHello
```

This returns the string "HelloHelloHello".

These two operators work well when you are working with only strings. If you want to use other data types, you can use the above examples by first passing your data into the function str(). In this way, you can add numbers to your constructed string. An example is shown in Listing 1-3.

Listing 1-3. Concatenating Non-Strings

```
>>> New_str = "Count = " + str(42)
>>> print(New_str)
Count = 42
```

1-2. Comparing Strings

Problem

You want to compare strings, checking to see whether two strings have the same value or checking to see whether two names point to the same string object.

Solution

There are two ways of doing comparisons, using is or using ==. The first is a way of testing whether two variable names refer to the same object, and the second is a way of comparing the actual value of each variable.

How It Works

To test if the same text is stored in two separate strings, use code like that in Listing 1-4.

Listing 1-4. Comparing Strings

```
str1 = "Hello"
str2 = "World"
if str1 == str2:
    print("The strings are equal")
else:
    print("The strings are not equal")
```

This code returns "The strings are not equal". You can use any of the usual comparison operators, like ! =, <, or >.

▪ **Note**   When doing a greater than or less than comparison, strings are compared letter by letter. Also, Python treats uppercase letters differently from lowercase letters. Uppercase letters come before lowercase letters, so Z comes before a.

1-3. Searching for a Substring
Problem

You want to search a string object for a substring.

Solution

You can detect whether a substring exists by using the in operator. You can locate the starting index for this substring by using the find() method of the string object.

How It Works

In Python, there is a polymorphic operator named in that you can use to see if one element of data exists within a larger set of data elements. This also works when you need to see if a substring exists within another string object. The usage is given in Listing 1-5.

Listing 1-5. Looking for a Substring

```
>>> Str1 = 'This is a string'
>>> 'is' in Str1
True
>>> 'me' in Str1
False
```

As you can see, it returns a Boolean value telling you whether the substring was found or not. If you need to instead find the location of a substring use the find method of the string object. Using the above code, you can look for a substring with

Listing 1-6. Finding the Index of a Substring

```
>>> Str1.find('is')
2
>>> Str1.find('me')
-1
```

This code returns the index for the first instance of the substring. If you want to find other instances, you can include a start and/or end index value over which to search. So, to find the second instance of is, use the code in Listing 1-7.

Listing 1-7. Finding a Substring Beyond the First One

```
>>> Str1.find('is', 3)
5
```

1-4. Getting a Substring

Problem

You need to get a substring from a string object.

Solution

Once you find the index for a substring, you can get it by copying out a slice of the original string. This is done by using the slice notation to grab the elements from the string.

How It Works

Slices are defined by a start index and an end index. To grab the first word in a string, you can use either of the options shown in Listing 1-8.

Listing 1-8. Slice Notation

```
>>> Str2 = 'One two three'
>>> Str2[0:2]
On
>>> Str2[:2]
On
>>> Str2[8:]
three
```

■ **Note**　Slices apply to all lists in Python. You can also use negative index values to count backwards, rather than forwards.

1-5. Replacing Text Matches

Problem

You need to replace a section of a string with new contents.

Solution

Since Python strings are immutable, replacing a substring involves chopping up the original string and then concatenating everything back together again into a new string.

How It Works

Let's use the above examples of slices and concatenation and put them together, as shown in Listing 1-9.

Listing 1-9. Manual String Replacement

```
>>> str1 = "Here are a string"
>>> corrected_str1 = str1[:5] + "is" + str1[7:]
>>> print(corrected_str1)
Here is a string
```

The string object includes a method called replace() that can also be used to replace one or more instances of a substring. You hand in the old substring, the new substring that you want to replace it with, and a count of how many instances to replace. See Listing 1-10.

Listing 1-10. Using the replace() Function

```
>>> corrected_str1 = str1.replace("are", "is", 1)
```

If the count is omitted, this method will replace every instance in the string.

1-6. Reversing a String
Problem

You need to reverse the contents of a string object.

Solution

Reversing a string can be done by using slice notation to select out the individual characters in reverse order.

How It Works

Python includes the idea of an extended slice, which contains a third parameter to define a stride length when moving across the list. If this stride length is negative, you are telling Python to step through the list backwards. The one-liner to reverse a string looks like the code in Listing 1-11.

Listing 1-11. Reversing a String with Slices

```
>>> str1 = "Hello World"
>>> str2 = str1[::-1]
>>> print(str2)
dlrow olleH
```

Since this is a special type of slice, you can use it to grab a substring and reverse it all in one command.

1-7. Trimming White Space
Problem

You need to trim whitespace from user input.

Solution

The strip() method of the string object can be used to delete any extraneous whitespace characters from a string.

How It Works

When your code needs to accept textual input from a user, you usually need to be able to trim away any whitespace characters that may exist at the beginning or the ending of the string. If you wish to simply remove every whitespace character from the beginning and ending of your string, you can use the strip() method. See Listing 1-12.

Listing 1-12. Stripping Whitespace

```
>>> str1 = "Space"
>>> str2 = str1.strip()
>>> print(str2)
Space
```

If there is a particular character that you want to strip from the beginning and ending of your string, you can hand it in as a parameter to the method. You can strip unwanted characters from either the beginning or the ending with the methods lstrip() or rstrip(), respectively.

1-8. Changing Case
Problem

You need to set the case of characters to either all uppercase or all lowercase.

Solution

Methods of the string object can perform case changes to the contents.

How It Works

Another issue that crops up when dealing with input from users is that you may need to set all of the characters to either uppercase or lowercase. This is often done to information that is being put into a database to simplify comparisons between two values. This way you avoid the previously mentioned issue where uppercase and lowercase characters are treated differently. In both cases, this is done with methods provided by the string object. See Listing 1-13.

Listing 1-13. Changing the Case of a String

```
>>> str1 = "Hello World"
>>> print(str1.lower())
hello world
>>> print(str1.upper())
HELLO WORLD
```

■ **Note**   You can capitalize a string with the method `capitalize()`.

1-9. Converting to Numbers
Problem

You need to convert user input numbers to a numeric data type.

Solution

There are cast functions available to change a string to some other data type. For numbers, there are the `int()`, `float()`, `long()`, and `complex()` functions.

How It Works

These functions take a string and they return a number of the type you requested. The string is expected to be of the same form as a numeric literal that would be entered directly in Python. If the string doesn't match the expected format for the requested type cast, you will get an error.

The default number base is 10. You can enter a different base so that you can create different numbers. For example, if you are entering hexadecimal numbers, you use the code in Listing 1-14.

Listing 1-14. Type Cast Functions

```
>>> hex1 = int("ae", 16)
>>> hex1
174
```

The possible bases are 2 to 36.

1-10. Iterating Over the Characters of a String

Problem

You need to iterate over the characters of a string object and apply some process for each character.

Solution

You can iterate over each character by using a `for` loop.

How It Works

If you need to process each of the individual characters of a given string, then you need to be able to iterate over that string. You can build a simple loop that uses indexing and pulls each element from the list. See Listing 1-15.

Listing 1-15. Iterating Over a String

```
str1 = "0123456789"
for i in range(10):
    print(str1[i], " and ")
```

This code returns the text "0 and 1 and 2 and 3". A more Pythonic way of doing this is to use an iterator. Happily, lists automatically support iterator methods. The code can be changed to that in Listing 1-16.

Listing 1-16. Using an Iterator

```
for i in str1:
    print(i, " and ")
```

1-11. Statistics on Texts

Problem

You need to find statistics on string objects.

Solution

If you are interested in looking at overall statistics for a given string, there are several different methods and functions available to collect this sort of information.

How It Works

The most basic statistic is the number of characters in your string, given by the function len(). You can find the minimum and maximum character values with the functions min() and max(). To get more detailed information, you can use the count() method to see how many times certain characters show up within your string. See Listing 1-17.

Listing 1-17. String Statistics

```
>>> str1 = "Hello world"
>>> len(str1)
11
>>> min(str1)
' '
>>> max(str1)
'w'
>>> str1.count('o')
2
```

1-12. Encoding Unicode
Problem

You need to encode a string as Unicode.

Solution

Python used to have a unicode data type for storing Unicode-encoded strings. Starting in version 3, Python string literals are stored as Unicode strings by default.

How It Works

If you are using Python 3, standard string objects are already stored as Unicode. If you are using Python 2, you can create them by using either the constructor or by defining a Unicode literal. See Listing 1-18.

Listing 1-18. Using Unicode

```
>>> ustr1 = unicode("Hello")
>>> ustr2 = u'Hello'
>>> ustr1 == ustr2
True
```

Unicode values are actually stored as integers. You can encode these values to a specific encoded string. For example,

```
ustr1.encode("utf-8")
```

gives you a new string encoded as UTF-8. You can also decode this string back into a normal Unicode string with the decode() method.

1-13. Translation

Problem

You need to translate the contents of a string.

Solution

You can apply a translation map to an entire string. This is handy if you want to accomplish several replacements.

How It Works

You can use the translate() method of your string to apply this mapping. While you could create the translation table manually, the string data type contains a helper function called maketrans() that creates a translation table that maps each character in the first parameter to the character at the same position in the second parameter. This is shown in Listing 1-19.

Listing 1-19. Translating Strings

```
>>> str1 = "Hello world"
>>> translate_table = str1.maketrans("abcd", "efgh")
>>> str1.translate(translate_table)
Hello worlh
```

The translate method optionally takes a second parameter that contains a set of characters to delete from the given string and to perform the translation. If you want to be able to just delete a set of characters from your string, you can do so by setting the translation table to None. In this way, you can get rid of the characters l and w with the code in Listing 1-20.

Listing 1-20. Using translate to Delete Characters

```
>>> str1.translate(str.maketrans({'l':None,'W':None}))
Heo ord
```

■ ■ ■

## CHAPTER 2

Numbers, Dates, and Times

The initial purpose of electronic computers was to calculate the answers to physical problems. This depended on the efficient use of numbers, and handling them correctly. This still consumed most of the CPU cycles spent in the average computer program. Along with dealing with numbers, there are many cases where you need to be able to handle dates and times. This gets a bit messy when you need to make comparisons between different time zones or across years with leap days.

2-1. Creating Integers

Problem

You need to create integers.

Solution

There are several ways to create integers. The simplest is to simply write an integer literal. There are also creation functions that allow you to make arbitrary integers with arbitrary bases. In Python, integers are numbers in an unlimited range, limited to the amount of memory available.

How It Works

Listing 2-1 shows an example.

Listing 2-1. Integer Literals

```
>>> a = 123456789
>>> a.bit_length()
27
```

This code creates a new integer object, accessed with the variable a. You can check to see how many bits are being used to store this integer with the method bit_length(). Integers are immutable, so if you try to change them by applying a mathematical operation, you will end up with a new integer.

© Joey Bernard 2016
J. Bernard, *Python Recipes Handbook*, DOI 10.1007/978-1-4842-0241-8_2

In Listing 2-2, you can see how to create integers using something other than base 10.

Listing 2-2. Integer Object Instantiation

```
>>> b = int('110',2)
>>> b
6
```

2-2. Creating Floating Points

Problem

You need to create floating point numbers.

Solution

As with integers, you can create floating point literals, or you can use the function float().

How It Works

When using floating point literals, you need to include either a decimal point or an exponent. See Listing 2-3 for some examples.

Listing 2-3. Using Float Literals

```
>>> b = 1.
>>> b
1.0
>>> c = 1e2
>>> c
100.0
```

The actual stored representation of a float is implementation-dependent and is different on different architectures.

2-3. Rounding Floats to Integers

Problem

You want to convert a floating point to an integer.

Solution

There are two ways to convert a floating point number to an integer. You can either truncate the number to just the portion before the decimal point, or you can round the number to the nearest integer value.

How It Works

You can use the same int() function as mentioned above. When you hand it a floating point as the input, it truncates the number towards 0. See Listing 2-4.

Listing 2-4. Truncating Floating Point Numbers

```
>>> c = 1234.567
>>> int(c)
1234
```

There is a function in the math module that will truncate floating point numbers to only the integer part. It's called math.trunc() and Listing 2-5 shows how to use it.

Listing 2-5. Using math.trunc()

```
>>> import math
>>> math.trunc(c)
1234
```

As you can see, it essentially chops off the fractional part and gives you the remaining portion. If you need to get a rounded value instead, check out Listing 2-6.

Listing 2-6. Rounding Floating Point Numbers

```
>>> round(c)
1235
```

If necessary, you can round to some fixed number of decimal places, as in Listing 2-7.

Listing 2-7. Rounding to One Decimal Place

```
>>> round(c, 1)
1234.6
```

2-4. Formatting Numbers

Problem

You need to get a string representation of a number.

Solution

The built-in function format() can be used to output various string representations of numbers.

How It Works

The format function takes a format specification that defines how your number should be converted into a string. The general format of such a string is shown in Listing 2-8.

Listing 2-8. Format Specification

```
[sign][width][.precision][type]
```

If the sign is +, your number will always have a leading sign. If it is -, a leading sign will only be added if the number is negative. If you use a space, you will get a leading minus sign if the number is negative or a leading space if the number is positive.

The width value defines a minimum size for the total number. If the width is larger than the size of the number, you will get leading spaces to pad it out to the correct size. The precision defines how many decimal spaces should be used when displaying your number. Of course, this is only valid for floating point numbers.

The type can be one of several different possibilities:

Type	Meaning
B	Binary format
D	Decimal integer
O	Octal integer
x	Hex format, using lowercase letters for a-f
X	Hex format, using uppercase letters for A-F
n	This is the same as d
None	This is the same as d

For floating point numbers, there is an entire other range of possible types available:

Type	Meaning
e	Exponential format, with e to mark the exponent. Default precision is 6.
E	Exponential format, with E to mark the exponent. Default precision is 6.
f	Fixed point with default precision 6.
F	Same as f, except nan is converted to NAN and inf to INF.
g	General format, where the number is rounded to the given precision. If the number is too large, then it is displayed in exponential form with e to mark the exponent. The default precision is 6.
G	This is the same as g, except the exponent is marked with E.
n	Number. This is the same as g except it uses the current locale to get the correct separator characters.

(continue)

Type	Meaning
%	Percentage, where the number is multiplied by 100, displayed in f format with a percentage sign.
None	This is the same as g.

Examples are shown in Listing 2-9.

Listing 2-9. Formatting Numbers

```
>>> format(c)
'1234.567'
>>> format(c, '+.2f')
'+1234.57'
>>> format(.25, '%')
'25.000000%'
```

2-5. Working with Arbitrary Precision Numbers

Problem

You need to work with floating point numbers that are of arbitrary size and precision.

Solution

Python provides a module called decimal that handles numbers of user-defined precision.

How It Works

The decimal module provides a new object called Decimal that abstracts the storage and manipulation of floating point numbers away from the underlying architecture. See Listing 2-10.

Listing 2-10. Importing the Decimal Object and Setting Precision

```
>>> from decimal import *
>>> getcontext()
Context(prec=28, rounding=ROUND_HALF_EVEN, Emin=-999999, Emax=999999,
capitals=1, clamp=0, flags=[], traps=[InvalidOperation, DivisionByZero,
Overflow])
>>> getcontext().prec = 10
```

Listing 2-10 shows how to set the precision used within the decimal module. Listing 2-11 shows how to use the Decimal class.

Listing 2-11. Using the Decimal Class

```
>>> a = Decimal(10.5)
>>> a
Decimal('10.5')
>>> 2*a
Decimal('21.0')
```

2-6. Generating Random Numbers

Problem

You need to generate random numbers in order to introduce randomization in your code.

Solution

The random module in Python provides functions to generate pseudo-random numbers for various distributions.

How It Works

Without very specialized hardware, all random numbers are generated using a class of functions called pseudo-random number generators (PRNGs). One of the better algorithms available is the class of functions called Mersenne twisters. The Python random module uses Mersenne twisters to generate random numbers. To initialize the generator, using the current system time as the seed, see Listing 2-12.

Listing 2-12. Initializing the Random Module

```
>>> import random
>>> random.seed()
```

You can get the next random floating point number between 0.0 and 1.0 by calling random.random(), as in Listing 2-13.

Listing 2-13. Getting the Next Random Number

```
>>> random.random()
0.35060766413719124
```

You can also make a random choice among a number of possibilities by using the random.choice() function, as in Listing 2-14.

Listing 2-14. Making a Random Choice

```
>>> items = [1, 2, 3, 4]
>>> random.choice(items)
3
```

16

2-7. Getting the Current Date and Time

Problem

You need to get the current date and time from the system.

Solution

Python provides a module called datetime that provides objects to handle dates, times, and time zones.

How It Works

The datetime module provides a datetime class that contains all of the date and time information, along with any time zone information. Listing 2-15 shows how to get the current date and time.

Listing 2-15. Getting the Current Date and Time

```
>>> import datetime
>>> curr_datetime = datetime.datetime.now()
>>> curr_datetime.year
2016
>>> curr_datetime.weekday()
2
```

There are many helper functions and attributes available in the datetime object that allow you to parse the date and time information in whatever way is needed.

If you only need the date or time portion, there are both date and time classes available. There are helper methods of the datetime class, namely date() and time(), that return objects of the appropriate type. Listing 2-16 shows how to get time and date objects for the current date and time.

Listing 2-16. Getting Objects for the Current Date and Time

```
>>> import datetime
>>> curr_datetime = datetime.datetime.now()
>>> curr_date = curr_datetime.date()
>>> curr_time = curr_datetime.time()
```

2-8. Calculating Date/Time Differences

Problem

You need to be able to find differences between two times and/or two dates.

Solution

Python provides the timedelta object as part of the datetime module.

How It Works

You can create a timedelta object that represents some date or time span. If you have two datetime objects, you can subtract them to get a timedelta object, as in Listing 2-17.

Listing 2-17. Finding the Difference Between Two Datetimes

```
>>> time1 = datetime.datetime.now()
>>> time2 = datetime.datetime.now()
>>> timediff = time2 - time1
>>> timediff.days
0
>>> timediff.seconds
7
>>> timediff.total_seconds()
7.532031
```

If you want to create a fixed timedelta, say one week, that you want to add to a given datetime object, you can create it and use it as in Listing 2-18.

Listing 2-18. Creating Timedeltas

```
>>> timediff = datetime.timedelta(days=7)
>>> time1 = datetime.datetime.now()
>>> time1.day
10
>>> time2 = time1 + timediff
>>> time2.day
17
```

2-9. Formatting Dates and Times

Problem

You need to generate string representations of the datetime object for display purposes.

Solution

The datetime object has a string format method that can generate a string defined by a specification string.

How It Works

The method strftime() takes a specification string and returns a string with the relevant values substituted in. A basic example is shown in Listing 2-19.

Listing 2-19. Formatting a Datetime String

```
>>> time3 = datetime.datetime.now()
>>> time3.strftime("%A %d. %B %Y %I:%M%p")
'Wednesday, 10. February 2016 09:39AM'
```

The possible formatting options are the following:

Directive	Meaning
%a	Weekday as locale abbreviated name
%A	Weekday as locale full name
%w	Day of week as a number between 0 and 6
%d	Day of month as a zero-padded number
%b	Month as locale abbreviated name
%B	Month as locale full name
%m	Month as a zero-padded number
%y	Year as a zero-padded two-digit number
%Y	Year as a zero-padded four-digit number
%H	Hour (24-hour clock) as a zero-padded number
%I	Hour (12-hour clock) as a zero-padded number
%p	Locale's equivalent of AM or PM
%M	Minute as a zero-padded number
%S	Second as a zero-padded number
%f	Microsecond as a zero-padded number
%z	UTC offset, in the form +HHMM or –HHMM
%Z	Time zone name
%j	Day of year as a zero-padded three-digit number
%U	Week of the year, using Sunday as the first day of the week
%W	Week of the year, using Monday as the first day of the week
%c	Locale's appropriate representation of the date and time
%x	Locale's appropriate representation of the date
%X	Locale's appropriate representation of the time
%%	Literal %

2-10. Reading Dates and Times from a String

Problem

You need to take user input and convert it into a datetime object.

Solution

The datetime class can instantiate a new object based on an input string.

How It Works

If you take in each of the elements of a date and time separately, you can use them directly in the datetime class, as in Listing 2-20.

Listing 2-20. Creating a Datetime Object

```
>>> date4 = datetime.datetime(year=1999, month=9, day=21)
>>> date4.weekday()
1
```

If you have an entire string, using a format of your own devising, you can use it within the strptime() function along with a format specification string. A simple example is given in Listing 2-21.

Listing 2-21. Using a Format String

```
>>> date5 = datetime.datetime.strptime("1999-09-21", "%Y-%m-%d")
>>> date5.weekday()
1
```

The format specification string takes the same signifiers as the strftime() function above.

CHAPTER 3

■ ■ ■

Iterators and Generators

Often you'll need to process some sequence of data from one source or another. The way to do this in Python is to use iterators. Many of the data types available in standard Python include an iterable interface that you can use. For those that don't, you can create a generator that then provides an iterable interface.

3-1. Iterating Over the Contents of a List

Problem

You want to iterate over the contents of a list.

Solution

While a list is iterable, you need to use the `iter` function to get access to the associated iterator.

How It Works

Listing 3-1 shows how to get access to the associated iterator for an iterable data type.

Listing 3-1. Accessing an Iterator

```
>>> my_list = [1, 2, 3, 4]
>>> new_iter = iter(my_list)
>>> new_iter
<list_iterator at 0x1ffb0b8e470>
```

You can use this new `iterator` object using the classic iterator techniques, as in Listing 3-2.

Listing 3-2. Using an Iterator

```
>>> next(new_iter)
1
>>> next(new_iter)
2
```

© Joey Bernard 2016
J. Bernard, *Python Recipes Handbook*, DOI 10.1007/978-1-4842-0241-8_3

Once you empty the `iterator`, you will get an exception raised, as in Listing 3-3.

Listing 3-3. Getting a StopIteration Exception

```
>>> next(new_iter)
4
>>> next(new_iter)
---------------------------------------------------------------------------
StopIteration                             Traceback (most recent call last)
<ipython-input-13-ed6082c80a14> in <module>()
----> 1 next(new_iter)

StopIteration:
```

3-2. Extracting the Contents of an Iterator

Problem

You need to enumerate an iterator to see what elements are contained within it.

Solution

The enumerate built-in function can take an `iterable` object and return a list of tuples containing a count and value.

How It Works

The enumerate built-in function takes an `iterable` object as the input, and returns tuples consisting of a count plus a value. The actual returned enumerate object is iterable itself, so you can use it as you would any other iterator. An example is shown in Listing 3-4.

Listing 3-4. Iterating Over an Enumerator

```
>>> pets = ['dogs', 'cats', 'lizards', 'pythons']
>>> pet_enum = enumerate(pets)
>>> next(pet_enum)
(0, 'dogs')
>>> next(pet_enum)
(1, 'cats')
```

By default, the count starts at 0. You can change this by using the start parameter, as in Listing 3-5.

Listing 3-5. Enumerating with a Different Count Start

```
>>> pet_enum2 = enumerate(pets, start=5)
>>> next(pet_enum2)
(5, 'dogs')
```

If you need all of the enumerated values at once for further processing, you can always create a list of the tuples with the code shown in Listing 3-6.

Listing 3-6. Making an Enumerated List

```
>>> pet_list = list(enumerate(pets))
>>> pet_list
[(0, 'dogs'), (1, 'cats'), (2, 'lizards'), (3, 'pythons')]
```

3-3. Filtering an Iterator

Problem

You need to filter out only selected items from an iterator.

Solution

The built-in `filter` function can selectively return only those elements that are true for some filtering function.

How It Works

The built-in `filter` function takes a filtering function as a parameter. This filtering function should return true for those elements of the iterator that you are interested in. In Listing 3-7, you see an example that returns the odd numbers from 0 to 9.

Listing 3-7. Getting the Odd Numbers Below 10

```
>>> odd_nums = filter(lambda x: x%2, range(10))
>>> next(odd_nums)
1
>>> next(odd_nums)
3
```

As you can see, `filter` returns an iterator that you can use in that fashion. If you need all of the elements in one go, you can always use the `list` function, shown in Listing 3-8.

Listing 3-8. Getting a List of Odd Numbers

```
>>> odd_list = list(filter(lambda x: x%2, range(10)))
>>> odd_list
[1, 3, 5, 7, 9]
```

If you want to use a negative filter, you need to use the `itertools` package. It includes the `filterfalse` function, which returns those elements that return false for some filtering function. Listing 3-9 shows how you can use this to get all of the even numbers.

Listing 3-9. Getting a List of Even Numbers

```
>>> import itertools
>>> even_list = list(itertools.filterfalse(lambda x: x%2, range(10)))
>>> even_list
[0, 2, 4, 6, 8]
```

We will ignore the argument as to whether 0 is an even number or not for this example.

3-4. Iterating Over the Contents of a File

Problem

You need to iterate over the contents of a file for processing.

Solution

The open function returns a file object that can be iterated over line by line for processing.

How It Works

The file object that is returned from the open function is an iterable object. The usual way to iterate over the contents is within a for loop, as in Listing 3-10.

Listing 3-10. Looping Over a File

```
>>> file1 = open('file.csv')
>>> for line in file1:
. . . : print(line)
. . ..:
1,one

2,two

3,three

4,four
```

The returned file object is actually an iterable function, however, so you can use it like any other iterator. Listing 3-11 shows an example.

Listing 3-11. Iterating Over a File

```
>>> file1 = open('file.csv')
>>> next(file1)
'1,one\n'
>>> next(file1)
'2,two\n'
```

3-5. Iterating Over Data That Has no Iterator

Problem

You need to create an iterable version of data that is not already iterable.

Solution

Many of Python's built-in data structures are already iterable, so there are fewer needs for generators. But, when you do need a generator, there is usually no other solution available.

How It Works

Essentially, any function that yields control back to the section where it was called from is a generator. Python understands that you intend to create a generator when you use the yield statement. It will automatically save the state of the function at the point of the yield statement so that you can return to it when next() is called. A simple example that generates the sequence of squares is shown in Listing 3-12.

Listing 3-12. Generating the Sequence of Squares

```
def squares(value=0):
    while True:
        value = value + 1
        yield (value-1)*(value-1)

>>> generator = squares()
>>> next(generator)
0
>>> next(generator)
1
>>> next(generator)
4
>>> next(generator)
9
```

New in Python 3.3 is the yield from statement. This is a way of creating a generator function that uses other iterators to generate the required values. For example, you can create a generator that counts up to some value and then back down again, as in Listing 3-13.

Listing 3-13. Generating a Count-Up Count-Down Function

```
def up_down(value=1):
    yield from range(1, value, 1)
    yield from range(value, 0, -1)
>>> list(up_down(3))
[1, 2, 3, 2, 1]
```

3-6. Creating Standard Classes of Iterators

Problem

When programming, there are several cases where you may have data structures that are best implemented as iterators of some type. In other words, you need to create one of the standard classes of iterators.

Solution

The itertools module provides a large selection of often used categories of iterators that you can use in many situations.

How It Works

There are general categories of iterators that can be very useful for many situations. For example, Listing 3-14 shows how to make an accumulator.

Listing 3-14. Creating an Accumulator

```
>>> import itertools
>>> accumulator = itertools.accumulate(range(10))
>>> next(accumulator)
0
>>> next(accumulator)
1
>>> next(accumulator)
3
>>> next(accumulator)
6
```

As a more complicated example, you can get all combinations of two numbers below 5 with the code in Listing 3-15.

Listing 3-15. Generating Combinations of Pairs

```
>>> list(itertools.combinations(range(5), 2))
[(0,1),
 (0, 2),
 (0, 3),
 (0, 4),
 (1, 2),
 (1, 3),
 (1, 4),
 (2, 3),
 (2, 4),
 (3, 4)]
```

CHAPTER 4

Files and I/O

For any type of data processing, files are absolutely necessary. It very quickly becomes the case that there is too much information to have the user input it manually. You need to be able to handle importing information directly from files of various types.

This chapter, you will look at the most common tasks you need to be able to handle in order to read and write files. You'll also look at how to deal with other forms of input and output.

4-1. Copying Files

Problem

You need to copy files from one location to another.

Solution

There are two functions from the shutil module that can be used to copy files.

How It Works

Copying files involves two parts of a file, the actual contents of said file and the metadata describing this file. Listing 4-1 shows how to only copy the contents of the file.

Listing 4-1. Copying File Contents

```
>>> import shutil
>>> new_file_path = shutil.copy('file1.txt', 'file2.txt')
```

This will copy file1.txt to file2.txt, returning the path of file2.txt to the variable new_file_path. If a directory name is given as the second parameter, the file will be copied into this directory using the original file name as the new filename. This function will also preserve the permissions of the file. If file1.txt is a symbolic link, this function call will create file2.txt as a separate file. If you want to actually create a copy of the symlink instead, you can use the example in Listing 4-2.

© Joey Bernard 2016
J. Bernard, *Python Recipes Handbook*, DOI 10.1007/978-1-4842-0241-8_4

Listing 4-2. Copying Symlinks

```
>>> shutil.copy('file1.txt', 'file2.txt', follow_symlinks=False)
```

If you want to preserve more of the metadata associated with the file, you can use copy2(), as shown in Listing 4-3.

Listing 4-3. Copying File Contents Plus Metadata

```
>>> shutil.copy2('file1.txt', 'file2.txt')
```

The amount of metadata that can be copied varies from operating system to operating system and platform to platform. It will copy as much as possible, with the worst case being that it can only do the same amount of work as copy(). Note that copy2() will never return a failure. It also accepts the follow_symlinks parameter, as does copy().

4-2. Moving Files
Problem
You need to move files from one location to another. This is also how you rename files, by moving them from one file name to another.

Solution
Because renaming and moving files is essentially the same thing to the filesystem, you can use either shutils.move() or os.rename() to achieve the same result.

How It Works
When using the move function, there is different behavior based on the location of the source and destination. If they are both on the same filesystem, the function os.rename() is used. Otherwise, a copying function is used to copy the file to the destination and then the source is removed. The default copying function is copy2, but you can hand in some other function, as shown in Listing 4-4.

Listing 4-4. Moving a File

```
>>> import shutil
>>> shutil.move('file1.txt', 'dir2', copy_function=copy)
```

The copying function needs to accept a source and a destination in order to be used by the move function.

If the files are on the same file system, you can use the rename function directly, as in Listing 4-5.

Listing 4-5. Renaming a File

```
>>> import os
>>> os.rename('file1.txt', 'dir2')
```

The major item to be aware of is that if the destination already exists and you have permission to write to it, it will be silently replaced with the source.

4-3. Reading and Writing Text Files

Problem

You need to open, read, and write text files.

Solution

You can use the built-in open function provided to open files, and then use the read and write methods to read from them and write to them.

How It Works

In Python, accessing files is done through a file descriptor object. This is the object that gets handed back as the returned object from a call to the built-in open function, as shown in Listing 4-6.

Listing 4-6. Opening a Text File for Reading

```
>>> fd1 = open('file1.txt')
>>> entire_file = fd1.read()
```

The file descriptor's read method will read in the entire contents of a file. This is not usually what you want to do. To read in some chunk of the file, you can hand in a size parameter, as in Listing 4-7.

Listing 4-7. Reading the First 100 Bytes of a File

```
>>> chunk1 = fd1.read(100)
```

Reading in data line by line is so common that there is a method provided to do just that. In Listing 4-8, you can see how to read in a single line, or how to loop through the entire file.

Listing 4-8. Reading a File Line by Line

```
>>> line1 = fd1.readline()
OR
>>> for line in fd1:
>>>     do_my_process(line)
```

If the file is not too large, you can read the entire contents into a list, where each element is a line from the file. Listing 4-9 provides an example.

Listing 4-9. Reading a File into a List

```
>>> file_list = fd1.readlines()
>>> first_line = file_list[0]
```

Writing a text file only requires a few minor changes. When calling the open function, the default is that you will be opening the file for reading only. In order to open the file for writing, you need to use a different mode. The modes of interest are as follows:

Mode	Description
w	Open the file for writing. If it already exists, truncate the contents to 0 size first.
a	Open the file for writing. If it already exists, move the insertion point to the end of the file, ready for appending.

4-4. Reading and Writing XML Files
Problem
You need to read in and process XML files, and then write out results.

Solution
The Python standard library includes an XML parser that generates an element tree that you can work with.

How It Works
The Python standard library includes an ElementTree class that provides a simplified way to work with XML structured data. To start, you need to open an XML file with the code in Listing 4-10.

Listing 4-10. Opening an XML File

```
>>> import xml.etree.ElementTree as ET
>>> my_tree = ET.parse('my_data.xml')
>>> root = my_tree.getroot()
```

Once you have the root element, you can query it and get the tag and attribute values, as in Listing 4-11.

Listing 4-11. Looking at Element Attributes

```
>>> root.tag
'tag value'
>>> root.attrib
{ }
```

You can easily iterate through the children of any given element. For example, Listing 4-12 shows how to iterate through all of the children of the root element.

Listing 4-12. Iterating Through the Children of the Root Element

```
for child in root:
    # look at the tag
    print(child.tag)
```

Elements can also be accessed as lists. This means that you can use list notations, as in Listing 4-13.

Listing 4-13. Getting the First Child of an Element

```
>>> child1 = root[0]
```

Altering an existing XML file, or creating a new one, is also very easy with the ElementTree class. You can directly change the text value of an element, and you can use the set() method to set element attributes. You can then use the write() method to save the changes. Listing 4-14 shows how to create a completely new XML file.

Listing 4-14. Creating a New XML File

```
>>> a = ET.Element('a')
>>> b = ET.SubElement(a, 'b')
>>> c = ET.SubElement(a, 'c')
>>> a.write('new_file.xml')
```

4-5. Creating a Directory
Problem

You need to create a new directory in which to write out files.

Solution

Python includes a new module called pathlib that provides an object-oriented way of working with paths.

31

How It Works

The core class for handling paths is Path. You need to start by creating a new Path object and setting the new directory name, as in Listing 4-15. You can then call the mkdir() method to create the actual new directory on the filesystem.

Listing 4-15. Creating a New Subdirectory

```
>>> from pathlib import Path
>>> p = Path('.')
>>> p.joinpath('subdir1')
>>> p.mkdir()
```

4-6. Monitoring a Directory for Changes

Problem

You need to monitor a directory and register when a change happens, like a new file is created.

Solution

The Path class includes a method to check the detailed properties of a directory or file.

How It Works

To check whether any changes have occurred in the current directory, you need to get the current status with the code in Listing 4-16.

Listing 4-16. Finding the Status of the Current Directory

```
>>> import pathlib
>>> p = pathlib.Path('.')
>>> modified_time = p.stat().st_mtime
```

You can then loop and see if this last modified time has changed. If so, then you know that the directory has changed. If you need to know what the change is, then you need to instead create a list of the contents and compare before and after the change is registered. You can generate a list of all of the current contents with the glob method, as in Listing 4-17.

Listing 4-17. Getting the Contents of a Directory

```
>>> import pathlib
>>> dir_list = sorted(pathlib.Path('.').glob('*'))
```

4-7. Iterating Over the Files in a Directory

Problem

You need to iterate over the contents of a directory in order to process a group of files.

Solution

The Path class includes a function to iterate over the contents, giving you a list of child Path objects.

How It Works

If you want to iterate over the contents of the current directory, you can use code like that in Listing 4-18.

Listing 4-18. Iterating Over the Contents of the Current Directory

```python
import pathlib
p = pathlib.Path('.')
for child in p.iterdir():
    # Do something with the child object
    my_func(child)
```

If you only want to work with files, you need to include a check, as in Listing 4-19.

Listing 4-19. Iterating Over the Files in the Current Directory

```python
import pathlib
for child in pathlib.Path('.').iterdir():
    if child.is_file():
        my_func(child)
```

4-8. Saving Data Objects

Problem

You need to save Python objects for future use in another Python program run.

Solution

Pickling objects is the standard way of serializing Python objects for later reuse.

How It Works

The Python standard library includes the module pickle. You need to open a file with the usual open function to hand it into the pickling functions. When you do open the file, you need to remember to include the binary flag. Listing 4-20 shows how to pickle a Python object to a file.

Listing 4-20. Pickling a Python Object

```
>>> import pickle
>>> file1 = open('data1.pickle', 'wb')
>>> pickle.dump(data_obj1, file1)
```

To reuse this data later, you can use the code in Listing 4-21 to reload it into Python.

Listing 4-21. Loading a Pickled Object

```
>>> file2 = open('data1.pickle', 'rb')
>>> data_reload = pickle.load(file2)
```

Don't forget to close the file handles after you are done.

4-9. Compressing Files

Problem

You need to compress a file to save space.

Solution

There are a number of modules available within the standard library to help you work with zip, gzip, bzip2, lzma, and tar files.

How It Works

To begin, let's look at how to work with zip files. The first step when working with compressed files is to open them. This is similar to the open function in Python, as in Listing 4-22.

Listing 4-22. Opening a Zip File

```
>>> import zipfile
>>> my_zip = zipfile.ZipFile('my_file.zip', mode='r')
```

The mode is used in the same way as in the open function. To read a currently existing zip file, you use mode 'r'. If you wish to create a new zip file to write to, you use mode 'w'. You can also modify an existing zip file by using mode 'a'.

You can add files to a zip file by using the write method, as in Listing 4-23.

Listing 4-23. Adding a File to a Zip Archive

```
>>> import zipfile
>>> my_zip = zipfile.ZipFile('archive1.zip', mode='w')
>>> my_zip.write('file1.txt')
>>> my_zip.close()
```

To extract files back out from an existing zip archive, use the code shown in Listing 4-24.

Listing 4-24. Extracting One File from a Zip Archive

```
>>> import zipfile
>>> my_zip = zipfile.ZipFile('archive1.zip', mode='r')
>>> my_zip.extract('file1.txt')
>>> my_zip.close()
```

You can extract everything with the method extractall(). If you don't know what files are in a given archive, you can get a listing with the method namelist().

If you need to work with the contents of a zip archive directly, you can read bytes from and write bytes to an archive. Once you have an opened zip file, you can read and write an archive with the code in Listing 4-25

Listing 4-25. Reading and Writing Bytes from a Zip Archive

```
>>> import zipfile
>>> my_zip = zipfile.ZipFile('file1.zip', 'a')
>>> data_in = my_zip.read('data1.txt')
>>> my_zip.write('data2.txt', data_out)
>>> my_zip.close()
```

Both the gzip and bzip2 modules handle compression of single files, as opposed to handling compressed archives of multiple files. To open either type, use the boilerplate code in Listing 4-26.

Listing 4-26. Opening Gzip or Bzip2 Files

```
>>> import gzip
>>> my_gzip = gzip.GzipFile('data1.txt.gz')
>>> import bz2
>>> my_bzip = bz2.BZ2File('data2.txt.bz')
```

In both cases, you get an object that implements BufferedIOBase. You can then read and write and manipulate the data within the compressed file. Remember to use the appropriate mode when creating a new gzip or bzip2 object.

CHAPTER 5

■ ■ ■

Python Data Analysis with pandas

One of the really big growth areas for Python is in the sciences, where data analysis is a huge component. Happily, Python includes a Swiss Army tool for data analysis, namely the pandas package, which can be installed from the PyPi repository with pip. pandas provides a lot of the data handling and data processing tools that you may be accustomed to if you come from an R background. Several new data types are introduced, along with additional functionality to handle the actual data processing in a very efficient manner. It achieves this efficiency by building on the functionality provided by the numpy package.

5-1. Working with 1D Data

Problem

You need to work with one-dimensional data such as arrays.

Solution

pandas includes a new data type called a Series that is used for one-dimensional data.

How It Works

Once you import the pandas package, you can use the Series constructor to take an already existing data object, such as a list, and convert it to a format that pandas can work with. Listing 5-1 shows how to convert a basic list.

Listing 5-1. Converting a List into a Series

```
>>> import pandas as pd
>>> data = [1,2,3,4]
>>> data_pd = pd.Series(data)
```

© Joey Bernard 2016   37
J. Bernard, *Python Recipes Handbook*, DOI 10.1007/978-1-4842-0241-8_5

You can optionally include an index array to index the values. In the example in Listing 5-1, the index simply becomes the numeric index within the data array. Also, by default, the data is left where it is. If you need to create a new copy of the data when you create your Series object, you can include the parameter copy=True. pandas can deduce the data type being used for the new Series object. You can explicitly set it with the dtype parameter. The possible values are those available from numpy. Listing 5-2 shows how you can treat the data from Listing 5-1 as floating point.

Listing 5-2. Explicitly Setting the dtype

```
>>> data_pd.dtype
dtype('int64')
>>> import numpy as np
>>> data_pd2 = pd.Series(data, dtype=np.float64)
>>> data_pd2.dtype
dtype('float64')
```

All of the usual operators are overloaded to be usable with Series objects, as in Listing 5-3.

Listing 5-3. Basic Arithmetic with Series

```
>>> 2 * data_pd
0    2
1    4
2    6
3    8
dtype: int64
```

Accessing elements is done with the same syntax as for lists, as in Listing 5-4.

Listing 5-4. Accessing Series Data

```
>>> data_pd[2]
3
>>> data_pd[3] = 9
```

5-2. Working with 2D Data
Problem

You need to work with two-dimensional data.

Solution

pandas includes an optimized object called a DataFrame that supports two dimensional data sets.

How It Works

pandas includes a new object called a DataFrame that creates an object for 2D data sets. You can create a new DataFrame from either a dictionary of lists, or from a list of dictionaries. Listing 5-5 shows how to create a new DataFrame from a dictionary of lists.

Listing 5-5. Creating a DataFrame

```
>>> d1 = {'one' : [1,2,3,4], 'two' : [9,8,7,6]}
>>> df1 = pd.DataFrame(d1)
>>> df1
   One  two
0   1    9
1   2    8
2   3    7
3   4    6
```

Again, the standard arithmetic operators are overloaded to be easy to use with DataFrames. Now that you have two dimensions, accessing elements is a bit more complicated. Addressing is column-based by default. This means that you can access a given column directly with the appropriate label, as in Listing 5-6.

Listing 5-6. Accessing DataFrame Columns

```
>>> df1['one']
0   1
1   2
2   3
3   4
Name: one, dtype: int64
>>> df1['one'][2]
3
```

If you want to access the data by row, you need to use either the iloc or loc properties of the DataFrame, as in Listing 5-7.

Listing 5-7. Accessing DataFrame Rows

```
>>> df1.loc[1]
one   2
two   8
Name: 1, dtype: int64
>>> df1.loc[1][1]
8
```

5-3. Working with 3D Data

Problem

You need to process three-dimensional data sets with pandas.

Solution

pandas includes a new object called a Panel that handles three-dimensional data sets efficiently.

How It Works

Similar to creating a DataFrame, creating a new Panel object can be done with a dictionary of DataFrames. Listing 5-8 shows a basic example.

Listing 5-8. Creating a Panel

```
>>> data_dict = {'item1' : pd.DataFrame(np.random.randn(4, 3)), 'item2' :
pd.DataFrame(np.random.randn(4, 2))}
>>> data_panel = pd.Panel(data_dict)
```

You can access each of the DataFrames within your new Panel by using their label. For example, you can get the item2 DataFrame with the code in Listing 5-9.

Listing 5-9. Accessing DataFrames within a Panel

```
>>> data_panel['item2']
           0          1    2
0 -2.126160 -0.677561 NaN
1 -2.110622 -1.535510 NaN
2 -0.387182 -1.412219 NaN
3 -0.370628  0.305436 NaN
```

Once you have a DataFrame, you can access individual elements in the same manner as in the previous section.

5-4. Importing Data from CSV Files
Problem

You need to import data collected offline from a CSV (comma-separated values) file.

Solution

Pandas includes a method named read_csv() that can import and parse CSV files.

How It Works

A top-level method is available in the pandas package to read in CSV files. The most basic usage is shown in Listing 5-10.

Listing 5-10. Reading a CSV File

```
>>> csv_data = pd.read_csv('data_file.csv')
```

By default, pandas will read the column names from the first row within the CSV file. If you have the column names on some other row, you can use the parameter header=X to redirect pandas to row X to pull the column names. If your file has no column names, you can use the parameter header=None and then hand in the list of column names with the parameter names=[col1, col2, …]. Also, by default, pandas will treat the first column as the labels for each of the rows. If the row labels are in another column, you can use the parameter index_col=X. If you don't have any row labels at all, you will probably want to use the parameter index_col=False to force pandas not to use any of the columns.

5-5. Saving to a CSV File
Problem

You want to save data into a CSV file to share with other people or applications.

Solution

The Series and DataFrame objects include a method called to_csv().

How It Works

If you need to save the data that you have been working with, you can call the to_csv() method with a file name to use, as in Listing 5-11.

Listing 5-11. Saving to a CSV File

```
>>> series_data.to_csv('export_file.csv')
```

There are parameters available to change the delimiter used or the character used for quoting. By default, pandas will write out column headers and row labels. If you want just the data, you can use the code in Listing 5-12.

Listing 5-12. Saving Data without Headers and Labels

```
>>> data2.to_csv('data_file.csv', header=False, index=False)
```

By default, pandas will overwrite the output file if it already exists. If you want to append to an already existing file, you can change the output mode with the parameter mode='a'.

5-6. Importing from Spreadsheets
Problem

You want to import existing data from a spreadsheet.

Solution

pandas includes a method to import a single sheet from a spreadsheet file, as well as a wrapper class if you need to work with more than one sheet from a given file.

How It Works

If you only need to import a single sheet from a file, you can use the code in Listing 5-13 to do so.

Listing 5-13. Importing a Single Spreadsheet Sheet

```
>>> data_frame1 = pd.read_excel('data_file.xsl', sheetname='Sheet1')
```

This will import the data as a single DataFrame object.

If you have multiple sheets that you wish to work with, it is more efficient to load the file once into a wrapper class in order to access them easily. Luckily, pandas has such a wrapper class, as shown in Listing 5-14.

Listing 5-14. Wrapping a Spreadsheet in pandas

```
>>> excel_data = pd.ExcelFile('data_file.xsl')
```

You can then hand this object in to the read_excel() method rather than a filename.

5-7. Saving to a Spreadsheet
Problem

You want to save your DataFrame to a spreadsheet file.

Solution

The DataFrame class includes a method named to_excel() that writes the data out to a file.

How It Works

The simplest way to write your output is shown in Listing 5-15.

Listing 5-15. Writing Output to a Spreadsheet File

```
>>> df.to_excel('output_file.xsl', sheet='Sheet1')
```

pandas will choose a different writing engine based on the file name extension. You can also save files using the file name ending .xslx.

5-8. Getting the Head and Tail

Problem

You want to query the data to see how it is structured.

Solution

There are functions available to look at the beginning or the ending of a given data set. They are very useful once you get to using large data sets.

How It Works

Both the Series and DataFrame objects have methods named head() and tail(). By default, they will give you the first five entries or the last five entries, respectively, for the given data set. If you want to look at more or less of the data, you can include a parameter for the number of entries you want to see, as in Listing 5-16.

Listing 5-16. Getting the First and Last Two Data Entries

```
>>> data_series = pd.Series(np.random.randn(1000))
>>> data_series.head(2)
0    -0.399614
1     1.307006
dtype: float64
>>> data_series.tail(2)
998     0.866424
999    -0.321825
dtype: float64
```

5-9. Summarizing Data

Problem

You want to get a statistical summary of the data set.

Solution

The new data objects introduced in pandas include a collection of methods used to provide summary statistics of your data.

How It Works

There are several methods available for individual statistics, such as the mean or standard deviation. There is also a single method called describe() that provides a complete summary, as shown in Listing 5-17.

Listing 5-17. Describing Your Data

```
>>> data_series.describe()
count     1000.000000
mean        -0.029861
std          0.990916
min         -3.261506
25%         -0.697940
50%         -0.048408
75%          0.646266
max          3.595167
dtype: float64
```

Each of these values is available with individual methods. For example, Listing 5-18 shows how you can verify that the standard deviation is equal to the square root of the variance.

Listing 5-18. Comparing the Standard Deviation and the Variance

```
>>> data_series.std() ** 2
0.9819137628988116
>>> data_series.var()
0.9819137628988115
```

This looks good, within the accuracy of floating point numbers.

5-10. Sorting Data
Problem

You wish to do some sorting as preprocessing of your data.

Solution

The Series and DataFrame objects include methods to sort either by index or by value.

How It Works

If your data is entered in a random order, you may need to do some preprocessing before you can do the actual analysis. Listing 5-19 shows how you can sort a DataFrame by either the row or column labels.

Listing 5-19. Sorting a DataFrame by Index

```
>>> df = pd.DataFrame({'one' : [1,2,3], 'two' : [4,5,6], 'three' : [7,8,9]},
index=['b','c','a'])
```

```
>>> df
    one  three  two
b    1     7    4
c    2     8    5
a    3     9    6
>>> df.sort_index()
    one  three  two
a    3     9    6
b    1     7    4
c    2     8    5
>>> df.sort_index(axis=1, ascending=False)
    two  three  one
b    4     7    1
c    5     8    2
a    6     9    3
```

The other way you may wish to sort your data is by the actual data values. In this case, you need to decide by which column to sort on. Listing 5-20 shows how to sort by column two in descending order.

Listing 5-20. Sorting a DataFrame by Values

```
>>> df.sort_values(by='two', ascending=False)
    one  three  two
a    3     9    6
c    2     8    5
b    1     7    4
```

■ **Note**   Starting with version 0.17.0, these methods return a new sorted object unless you use the parameter `inplace=True`. Before this version, the sorting happens in the original data object.

5-11. Applying Functions Row- or Column-Wise
Problem

You need to execute a function on an entire row or column.

Solution

Both `DataFrames` and `Panels` have a method called `apply()` that can be used to apply a function across a column or row.

How It Works

Listing 5-21 shows how you can find the average for each column, then each row.

Listing 5-21. Averaging Rows and Columns

```
>>> df = pd.DataFrame({'one' : [1,2,3], 'two' : [4,5,6], 'three' : [7,8,9]},
index=['b','c','a'])
>>> df.apply(np.mean)
one      2.0
three    8.0
two      5.0
dtype: float64
>>> df.apply(np.mean, axis=1)
b    4.0
c    5.0
a    6.0
dtype: float64
```

This is a great place to use lambda functions, if your function is simple enough to fit into a single expression. Listing 5-22 shows an example of a simple lambda function that simply doubles the values from the dataframe.

Listing 5-22. Applying a Lambda Function on a Data Set

```
>>> df.apply(lambda x: 2*x, axis=1)
   one  three  two
b   2     14     8
c   4     16    10
a   6     18    12

[3 rows x 3 columns]
```

5-12. Applying Functions Element-Wise
Problem

You need to apply functions to either all of the elements in a data set or some subset of the elements.

Solution

The new pandas data objects have two useful methods named `map()` and `applymap()` that can be used to apply functions to groups of individual elements.

How It Works

There are times when you need to apply some function to individual elements of your data set. Listing 5-23 shows how you can square all of the elements of a data set.

Listing 5-23. Squaring Data Elements

```
>>> df = pd.DataFrame({'one' : [1,2,3], 'two' : [4,5,6], 'three' : [7,8,9]},
index=['b','c','a'])
>>> df.applymap(lambda x: x*x)
   one   three  two
b   1      49   16
c   4      64   25
a   9      81   36
```

If you only wish to apply a function to a given column, Listing 5-24 shows how you can double the values in column 2.

Listing 5-24. Doubling a Single Column of Elements

```
>>> df['two'].map(lambda x: 2*x)
b     8
c    10
a    12
Name: two, dtype: int64
```

5-13. Iterating Over Data
Problem

You need iterate over your data set as part of the processing workflow.

Solution

pandas data objects are iterable objects and can be used in most cases when you need to loop over all of the elements.

How It Works

If you want to do basic iteration of one of the new data objects that pandas provides, you need to be aware that they each behave a little differently. The basic types of iteration are

- Series: Iterate over each element
- DataFrame: Iterate over the columns
- Panel: Iterate over the item labels

For example, Listing 5-25 shows how to find the average of each column using iteration.

Listing 5-25. Averaging Each Column of a DataFrame

```
>>> df = pd.DataFrame({'one' : [1,2,3], 'two' : [4,5,6], 'three' : [7,8,9]},
index=['b','c','a'])
>>> for col in df:
....:        print(df[col].mean())
....:
2.0
8.0
5.0
```

If you need to iterate over the rows of a DataFrame instead, Listing 5-26 shows one example.

Listing 5-26. Iterating Over Rows

```
>>> for row_index,row in df.iterrows():
....:        print(row_index)
....:        print(row)
....:
b
one      1
three    7
two      4
Name: b, dtype: int64
c
one      2
three    8
two      5
Name: c, dtype: int64
a
one      3
three    9
two      6
Name: a, dtype: int64
```

Note, however, that iterating can be rather slow. Whenever possible, you will probably want to find another way of expressing the processing workflow that you need to do.

CHAPTER 6

Functions

Any modern programming language needs to have some way of combining functionality into reusable chunks of code. In Python, one of the most basic units of reusable code is the function. In this chapter, you will look at how functions work within Python, as well as some places where they may do something surprising.

6-1. Creating Basic Functions

Problem

You want to create a basic function to handle a simple task, such as finding the square of two.

Solution

Within Python, you can use the built-in def keyword to create a new function.

How It Works

Listing 6-1 shows an example.

Listing 6-1. Defining a Basic Function

```
def square_of_two():
    ans = 2 * 2
    return ans
```

As you can see, the body of the function's code is defined by the indentation level. The first line uses def and creates a new function with the given name. In this case, you create a function called square_of_two(). You can now call this function as you would any other. For an example, see Listing 6-2.

© Joey Bernard 2016
J. Bernard, *Python Recipes Handbook*, DOI 10.1007/978-1-4842-0241-8_6

Listing 6-2. Calling a Function

```
>>> square_of_two()
4
>>> my_ans = square_of_two()
```

If your function is supposed to return a value to the calling statement, then you need to use the built-in return keyword. If you have conditionals or loops within your new function, you will need to increase the indentation level for these structures, as in Listing 6-3.

Listing 6-3. Factorial of Two Function

```
def fact_two():
    a = 2
    ans = a
    while a > 1:
        ans = ans * (a-1)
        a = a - 1
    return ans
```

This returns the factorial of 2, which is 2.

6-2. Using Named Parameters Rather Than Positional Parameters

Problem

You want to hand in parameters to your function, optionally using names. This allows for parameters being handed in to your function in an arbitrary order.

Solution

Since variable names are untyped in Python, you simply need to add names to the parameter list within the parentheses. These can be used based on position or they can be explicitly by name.

How It Works

Adding parameters can be done very simply, as in Listing 6-4.

Listing 6-4. Squaring Any Number

```
def square_num(a):
    return a*a
```

You can then call this function two different ways, either by position or by label. Listing 6-5 shows what this would look like.

Listing 6-5. Calling Functions with Parameters

```
>>> square_num(2)
4
>>> square_num(a=3)
9
```

If you have more than one parameter, you can mix the use of positional and named parameters. The only thing to be aware of is that all positional parameters need to be included before using any named parameters. Listing 6-6 shows a simple example.

Listing 6-6. Multiplying Many Numbers

```
def multiplication(a, b, c):
    return a*b*c
>>> multiplication(1, 2, 3)
6
>>> multiplication(2, c=3, b=1)
6
```

If you try something like multiplication(1, a=2, c=3), you will get an error because by positional rules you have already given *a* a value, and then you try to give it another value with the named parameter a=2. Also, if you try to use a positional parameter after a named parameter, such as multiplication(a=1,b=2,3), you will also get an error.

6-3. Using Default Values in Functions
Problem

You want to allow a function to use default values if none are handed in.

Solution

When a function and its input parameters are defined, you can include a default value to use if none are provided.

How It Works

You can simply state what the default values need to be when you define the function, as in Listing 6-7.

Listing 6-7. Defining Default Parameter Values

```
def multiplication(a=1,b=2,c=3):
    return a*b*c
```

All of the rules around positional and named parameters still apply. Listing 6-8 shows some examples.

Listing 6-8. Multiplication Examples

```
>>> multiplication()
6
>>> multiplication(5)
30
>>> multiplication(1,1)
3
>>> multiplication(c=1)
2
```

Now that you have default values, you have actions that can happen invisibly to someone who has not read the code for themselves. In this case, it makes sense to switch to using strictly named parameters to help clarify the code and to aid in future code maintenance.

6-4. Implementing a Recursive Algorithm
Problem

You need to implement a recursive algorithm within your Python program.

Solution

Python supports recursion, so you can call a function from within itself.

How It Works

Since Python supports recursion, you can simply call a function directly. The classic example is calculating a factorial, as in Listing 6-9.

Listing 6-9. Calculating Factorials Through Recursion

```
def fact(a):
    if a == 1:
        return 1
    else:
        return a * fact(a-1)
>>> fact(5)
120
```

While there are some algorithms that only really work as a recursive function, they should be approached warily. Recursive functions actually are nested function calls. This means that each step through the recursion needs to push the current state onto the stack before the next call. You can very quickly use up large amounts of RAM, depending on what needs to be tracked. Also, each function call requires more time to do the context switch. So always be sure that this is the only solution before diving into a recursive function.

6-5. Using Lambda Functions to Create Temporary Anonymous Functions

Problem

You need a function temporarily (as a parameter for another function, for example) and don't need it accessible by name.

Solution

Python has the mechanism of the built-in lambda statement, which provides the ability to create and use anonymous functions.

How It Works

To show how you can use lambda functions, we need an example that requires one. Listing 6-10 shows a function that takes two parameters and a function, and executes the given function with the two given parameters as input.

Listing 6-10. Applying a Function

```
def apply_operator(a, b, f):
    return f(a,b)
```

If you want to just use a one-off function in the above example code, you can use a lambda function directly within the call. Listing 6-11 shows how to apply a multiplication function.

Listing 6-11. Applying a Multiplication Function

```
>>> apply_operator(2, 3, lambda x, y: x*y)
6
```

The big limitation with lambda functions is that they are restricted to a single expression line. Anything larger than that needs to be defined as a regular function.

6-6. Generating Specialized Functions

Problem

You need to create a function that can generate specialized functions for special cases. For example, you might want a different averaging function for complex numbers rather than for regular floating point numbers.

Solution

Using lambda functions, you can generate specialized functions.

How It Works

Since functions are simply another type of object, they can be returned from a function call. Using this fact, you can create a function that takes in some input parameter and kicks out a function defined by it. For example, Listing 6-12 generates a scaling function based on an input value.

Listing 6-12. Generating Scaling Functions

```
def generate_scaler(a):
    return lambda x: a*x
```

You can then use this generator to create a function that scales numbers by 2 or 3, as in Listing 6-13.

Listing 6-13. Function Generator Examples

```
>>> doubler = generate_scaler(2)
>>> doubler(3)
6
>>> tripler = generate_scaler(3)
>>> tripler(3)
9
```

CHAPTER 7

Classes and Objects

Once you have a way of storing blocks of code into reusable functions, it is a natural progression to want to bundle multiple functions together into larger blocks of reusable code called *objects*. Along with this actual code, you may also want to store data in the form of *properties*. In order to define these new objects, you need to create classes and then instantiate them into actual objects that you can use. In this chapter, you will look at some of the most common tasks that come up when you start defining and using new objects.

7-1. Discovering the Type of an Object (Everything Is an Object)
Problem

Just about everything in Python is an object. The important thing is to find out what kind of object you have in your possession.

Solution

The built-in function type() returns the class of the object handed in as the parameter. You can also use isinstance() to test whether the given object is of the same type of some particular class.

How It Works

Listing 7-1 shows an example.

Listing 7-1. Checking the Type of an Object

```
>>> a = 1
>>> type(a)
<class 'int'>
>>> b = "Hello World"
>>> type(b)
<class 'str'>
```

© Joey Bernard 2016
J. Bernard, *Python Recipes Handbook*, DOI 10.1007/978-1-4842-0241-8_7

This will query the given object and return a type object for the inputted object. You can use this to check if two objects are of the same class. If you want to see if an object is of a particular class, you can use isinstance(), as in Listing 7-2.

Listing 7-2. Is an Object of a Particular Class?

```
>>> a = 1
>>> isinstance(a, int)
TRUE
```

7-2. Creating Classes
Problem

You wish to create a new class, encapsulating a set of methods and attributes, to use in other pieces of code.

Solution

The class keyword allows you to define a new class.

How It Works

As with functions, defining a new class is as simple as using the class keyword and then having an indented block of code. You can see a very simple example in Listing 7-3.

Listing 7-3. Creating a Simple Class

```
class my_simple_class:
    a = 3
    b = "Hello World"
```

Listing 7-4 shows a more complex example that includes a series of methods, too.

Listing 7-4. Creating a Complex Class

```
class my_complex_class:
    a = 42
    def method1():
        print("The value of a is " + str(a))
    b = "Hello World"
```

7-3. Adding Private Fields
Problem

You wish to have some parts of your class private—that is, not accessible from other pieces of code.

Solution

In Python, all methods and attributes are publicly visible. As a solution, the addition of underscore characters to the name of the attribute or method is nearly universally accepted as representing an element that is not meant for public consumption.

How It Works

Defining an attribute that is meant to be only used within the class in question should be prefixed with at least one underscore character. The usual way this is done is to actually add two underscore characters to both the beginning and ending of the element names, as in Listing 7-5.

Listing 7-5. Creating a Private Variable

```
class priv_vars:
    __a__ = "This is a private variable"
```

There is a special form of a private name that induces Python to rename the element using a system of name mangling. If you have an element that may have the same name as some other element, you can add at least two leading underscore characters and at most one trailing underscore. Python will then prepend the class name to the element name. For example, if you had a class like

```
class my_class1:
    __a_ = 1
```

the attribute __a_ would be renamed as _my_class__a_ in order to avoid name collision.

7-4. Subclassing
Problem

You want to build on the functionality provided in another class.

Solution

The ability to subclass is key to any object-oriented programming language. Python supports inheritance from either a single base class or a multiple of base classes.

How It Works

Inheriting from a class is a simple matter of adding a reference to the class in question in the definition of your new class. A simple example is given in Listing 7-6.

Listing 7-6. Inheriting from a Class

```
class animal:
    type = "mammal"
class dog(animal):
    breed = "labrador"
>>> my_dog = dog()
>>> my_dog.breed
labrador
>>> my_dog.type
mammal
```

As you can see, the class dog inherits the attribute of the animal type. The way methods and attributes are resolved is that the main class is checked first to see if it exists there. If it doesn't, then Python will check any inherited class to see if the attribute or method exists there. This means that you can override inherited methods or attributes with your own version. In Listing 7-7, the animal type is changed to bird.

Listing 7-7. Overriding Class Attributes

```
class bird(animal):
    type = "bird"
>>> my_bird = bird()
>>> my_bird.type
bird
```

If you are inheriting from multiple classes, you can simply add them as multiple parameters in your class definition, as in Listing 7-8.

Listing 7-8. Multiple Inheritance

```
class eagle(animal, bird):
    species = "eagle"
>>> my_eagle = eagle()
>>> my_eagle.type
animal
```

As you can see, order matters when dealing with multiple inheritances. When Python tries to resolve where a method or attribute is defined, it begins with the main class and then continues through the inherited classes in order from left to right until it finds the first instance of said method or attribute. In the above case, the correct order of inheritance should be class eagle(bird, animal).

7-5. Initializing Objects
Problem

You need to have some initial values or initial processing steps executed when a new object is instantiated.

Solution

You can use the private method __init__ to run setup code at initialization.

How It Works

When Python instantiates a new object, it looks to see if there is a method called __init__. If it finds it, this function is executed as soon as the instantiation is finished. It can also take parameters at instantiation time that can be used to further handle setup steps, as in Listing 7-9.

Listing 7-9. Initialization Functions

```
class my_complex:
    def __init__(self, real_part, imaginary_part):
        self.r = real_part
        self.i = imaginary_part

>>> complex_num = my_complex(2, 3)
>>> complex_num.r
2
```

The parameter self refers to the object being instantiated, allowing you to interact with the object during initialization.

7-6. Comparing Objects
Problem

You need to compare two objects to see if they are the same.

Solution

When comparing objects, there are two different ideas of equality: comparing an object to itself and seeing if two different objects have the same attributes.

How It Works

The first type of equality is to test whether two variable names are actually pointing to the same object. This is a side effect of the separation between objects and the labels that point to them within Python. To test for this type of equality, you need to use the operators is and is not, as in Listing 7-10.

Listing 7-10. Comparing Object Identities

```
>>> a = "string1"
>>> b = a
>>> a is b
True
```

The next type of comparison involves comparing the contents of two objects to see if they have the same value. The concept of value is not a general concept in Python. The calculation of object value is handled by the operator code executed when you use the operators ==, !=, <=, >=, <, and >. Depending on the details of any classes that you have defined, you may want to override the code for these comparison operators. For example, let's say that you have created a class that represents a book and you wish to use the number of pages as the value of a given book object. You can then override the operators with the code in Listing 7-11.

Listing 7-11. Overriding Comparison Operators

```
class book:
    def __init__(self, pages):
        self.pages = pages
    def __lt__(self, other):
        return self.pages < other
    def __gt__(self, other):
        return self.pages > other
....
```

and so on, for all of the operator methods.

7-7. Changing an Object After Creation
Problem
You need to change an object after it has been created.

Solution
Within Python, almost all objects are malleable and can be altered in terms of their attributes and methods. Built-in objects, like str or int, aren't malleable. Objects that are created from your own class definitions are malleable and can have new attributes dynamically created and used.

How It Works
As an example, you can add the title of your books, using the class defined in Listing 7-11, by simply using a new attribute named title, as in Listing 7-12.

Listing 7-12. Dynamically Created Attributes

```
>>> book1 = book(42)
>>> book1.title = "My Book"
>>> book1.title
My Book
```

You can use this malleability to create really fast, flexible data structures by defining a class that doesn't do anything, as in Listing 7-13.

Listing 7-13. Empty Classes for Data Storage

```
class my_container:
    pass
>>> container1 = my_container()
>>> container1.label = "The first container"
>>> container1.phone = "555-5555"
>>> container1.name = "John Doe"
```

The keyword pass is a no-op function. It essentially takes up space where an expression is supposed to go, but tells Python that there is not actually any code to run. This lets you create a completely empty object that you can then add to later.

7-8. Implementing Polymorphic Behavior
Problem

You need to include behavior that changes depending on what inputs are being given.

Solution

Python handles polymorphism through the fact that it is a duck-typed language. Basically, when a function tries to use an object as a parameter, it will actually get the value from the object through some standard method that the object needs to implement.

How It Works

The best way to show this technique is to use an example. Listing 7-14 shows a series of classes and functions to be used in this example.

Listing 7-14. Polymorphic Classes and Methods

```
class dog:
    def talk(self):
        print("bark")
```

```
class cat:
    def talk(self):
        print("meow")

def speak(animal):
    animal.talk()
```

From here, you will get different behavior from the function speak() based on which type of animal you hand in as a parameter. Listing 7-15 shows an example of this varying behavior.

Listing 7-15. Polymorphic Behavior

```
>>> my_dog = dog()
>>> my_cat = cat()
>>> speak(my_dog)
bark
>>> speak(my_cat)
meow
```

CHAPTER 8

■ ■ ■

Metaprogramming

One of the key mantras in programming is to not repeat yourself. Whenever you do the same task more than once, you should take a look at it to see if there is any way to automate it. This is the primary reason for writing programs. But this applies equally to the task of writing the code itself. If you are repeating chunks of code, you should step back to see if there is some better way of achieving the same result.

One technique available to deal with this issue is metaprogramming. Essentially, metaprogramming is code that affects other code. The usual way this is done within Python is either with decorators, metaclasses, or descriptors.

8-1. Using a Function Decorator to Wrap Existing Code

Problem

You want to alter the behavior of an already existing function by wrapping it with other code. This wrapper code can then be swapped in or out from different modules if they use the same decorator name, allowing you to alter the original function in different ways.

Solution

A function can be wrapped by adding a decorator to the top of the function definition, using a label that begins with an ampersand.

How It Works

Listing 8-1 shows an example where you use the decorators provided by the line_profile module.

© Joey Bernard 2016
J. Bernard, *Python Recipes Handbook*, DOI 10.1007/978-1-4842-0241-8_8

Listing 8-1. Using the Profile Decorator

```
from line_profile import *

@profile
def my_adder(x, y):
    return x + y
```

This code wraps the function my_adder() with profiling code from the line_profile module. This module is not part of the standard library, so you need to install it onto your system. This is the same as explicitly wrapping one function with another, as in Listing 8-2.

Listing 8-2. Wrapping a Function

```
from line_profiler import *

def my_adder(x, y):
    return x + y

my_adder = profile(my_adder)
```

8-2. Writing a Function Decorator to Wrap Existing Code

Problem

You want to write a wrapper for a function to add extra functionality.

Solution

Python includes the wraps keyword that defines a function that can wrap another function and be used as a decorator.

How It Works

In order to write a decorator of your own, you need to use the wraps keyword from the functools module. This keyword is used as a decorator to help define your own new decorator. Listing 8-3 shows an example that prints out the function name of the decorated function.

Listing 8-3. A Decorator to Print Out Function Names

```
from functools import wraps
def function_name(func):
    message = func.__qualname__
    @wraps(func)
    def wrapper((*args, **kwargs)):
        print(message)
        return func(*args, **kwargs)
    return wrapper
```

You can then use it just like any other decorator, as in Listing 8-4.

Listing 8-4. Using Your Own Decorator

```
@function_name
def adder(x,y):
    return x+y
```

8-3. Unwrapping a Decorated Function
Problem

You need to get access to the functionality of a function that has been decorated.

Solution

You can get the original unwrapped function by using the __wrapped__ attribute of the function.

How It Works

Assuming that the decorator was correctly coded using the wraps function from functools, then you can get the original function by using the __wrapped__ attribute, as in Listing 8-5.

Listing 8-5. Getting the Unwrapped Function

```
>>> adder(2,3)
adder
5
>>> adder.__wrapper__(2,3)
5
```

8-4. Using a Metaclass to Change the Construction of a Class

Problem

You need to add extra functionality to a class, similar to a decorator for functions. This can be done by changing what object a class is an instance of by using a metaclass.

Solution

Metaclasses can be used in a similar fashion to using subclasses.

How It Works

When using a metaclass, you include it in the class definition, as in Listing 8-6.

Listing 8-6. Using a Metaclass

```
class my_counter(metaclass=Singleton):
    pass
```

By default, a class is an instance of the type class. The code in Listing 8-6 makes the new class an instance of the Singleton class rather than the type class. You can also set the metaclass within the class definition, as in Listing 8-7.

Listing 8-7. Setting the __metaclass__ Attribute

```
class my_counter():
    __metaclass__ = Singleton
    pass
```

In both Listing 8-6 and 8-7, your new class is created as an instance of the Singleton class. This is one method of using the singleton design pattern within Python.

8-5. Writing a Metaclass

Problem

You need to change how a class is instantiated by writing your own metaclass.

Solution

With the use of a metaclass, you can redefine how a class is actually instantiated, allowing you to create classes that can only be instantiated once (the singleton design pattern), or are cached, for example. These examples are used for logging classes or streaming data parsers.

How It Works

You create a metaclass by building a class that overwrites one or more of the functions used during instantiation. For example, you could override the __call__ function to create a class that cannot be instantiated, as in Listing 8-8.

Listing 8-8. A Metaclass That Stops Instantiation

```
class CannotInit(type):
    def __call__(self, *args, **kwargs):
        raise TypeError("Cannot instantiate")
```

Now, when you try to use it as a metaclass and directly instantiate the new class, you will get an exception raised.

If you need more complicated behavior, as in a singleton, for example, you can override multiple functions, as in Listing 8-9.

Listing 8-9. Creating a Singleton Metaclass

```
class MySingleton(type):
    def __init__(self, *args, **kwargs):
        self.__instance = None
        super().__init__(*args, **kwargs)

    def __call__(self, *args, **kwargs):
        if self.__instance is None:
            self.__instance = super().__call__(*args, **kwargs)
            return self.__instance
        else:
            return self.__instance
```

This code traps the both the instantiation and the calling of any class that uses this metaclass so that only one instance can exist at a single time.

8-6. Using Signatures to Change the Parameters a Function Accepts

Problem

You want to be able to control the signature for a function at runtime. This allows you to dynamically change what parameters a function accepts. For example, you can force your function to only use keyword parameters in one case, and then allow for positional or keyword parameters in another case.

Solution

The inspect module includes the tools needed to create and use signatures for functions.

How It Works

The example in Listing 8-10 shows how to create a new signature.

Listing 8-10. Creating a Signature

```
>>> from inspect import Signature, Parameter
>>> params = [Parameter('x', Parameter.POSITIONAL_OR_KEYWORD),
...              Parameter('y', Parameter.POSITIONAL_OR_KEYWORD, default=42),
...              Parameter('z', Parameter.KEYWORD_ONLY, default=None)]
>>> my_sig = Signature(params)
>>> print(my_sig)
(x, y=42, *, z=None)
```

In this code, you use the `Parameter` class to create a list of function parameters. There are keywords for each type of parameter. One thing to note is that if you have a list of keyword-only parameters in a normal function definition, you use an asterisk to mark which parameters are keyword only. This shows up when you print out the newly created signature.

To use this signature, you can use the `bind` method to take the generic lists of positional and keyword parameters and bind them to the parameters within the signature you created. An example is given in Listing 8-11.

Listing 8-11. Using a Signature

```
def my_func(*args, **kwargs):
    bound_values = my_sig.bind(*args, **kwargs)
    for name, value in bound_values.arguments.items():
        print(name, value)
```

This way, you can have the same function bind the parameters using different signatures, based on how you need to process them.

CHAPTER 9

■ ■ ■

Networking and the Internet

The Internet has completely changed how we use computers. Before, we focused on what we could do with the hardware on our desks; now we can think about what work can be done on machines distributed across the globe. In this chapter, you will learn some of the core techniques for communicating with other machines over networks, such as the Internet. You'll begin by looking at one of the lowest level methods: using sockets. The rest of the recipes will look at higher-level techniques that hide much of the complexity surrounding Internet communications.

9-1. Opening a Socket Connection
Problem

You want to open a raw network socket connection to handle unstructured data communication.

Solution

The Python standard library includes a socket class that exposes the low-level interface for network communications.

How It Works

The socket class provides a way of accessing the network hardware at an extremely low level. As such, it has to support many different networking protocols. For these recipes, you will be focusing on the most common situation, that of wanting to create a TCP/IP socket over an Ethernet connection. The socket module contains the socket class and several other utility functions and classes that you can use. Listing 9-1 shows how to create a new socket and connect to a remote machine.

Listing 9-1. Opening a Socket to a Remote Machine

```
import socket
host = '192.168.0.1'
port = 5050
```

© Joey Bernard 2016
J. Bernard, *Python Recipes Handbook*, DOI 10.1007/978-1-4842-0241-8_9

```
my_sock = socket.socket(socket.AF_INET, socket.SOCK_STREAM)
my_sock.connect((host, port))
```

In this code, the machine address is given as a string containing an IP address and the port is given as a number. This instantiation method creates a socket object that can be used for either making outgoing connections to a remote machine or for listening for incoming connection requests from those remote machines. If you are strictly interested in only making an outgoing connection to a remote machine, you can instead use the create_connection() method, as in Listing 9-2.

Listing 9-2. Making an Outgoing Socket Connection

```
import socket
host = '192.168.0.1'
port = 5050
my_sock = socket.create_connection((host, port))
```

This newly created socket object can now be used to send data to and receive data from the remote machine. When you are done with a given socket connection, do not forget to close it down so that the operating system can cleanly shut down the connection and clean up after it. Listing 9-3 shows the boilerplate code to do so.

Listing 9-3. Closing a Socket Connection

```
my_sock.close()
```

9-2. Reading/Writing Over a Socket
Problem

You want to communicate with a remote machine over an open socket connection.

Solution

The socket class contains a number of different methods for both sending and receiving data over a socket connection.

How It Works

Once a socket has been opened, you can use methods from the socket object to send and receive data. The most basic way to send data is to use the send() method, as in Listing 9-4.

Listing 9-4. Sending Data Over a Socket

```
msg = b'Hello World'
mesglen = len(msg)
totalsent = 0
```

```
while totalsent < msglen:
    sent = my_sock.send(msg[totalsent:])
    totalsent = totalsent + sent
```

There are a few things to note here. First, sockets send bytes across the network, so your message needs to be a byte string. The second thing to note is that the send() method does not make any guarantees as to how much of your data will get sent during any particular call. All it does do is return the number of bytes that were successfully sent on any particular call, hence the need for a while loop to continue sending until you are sure that everything was transmitted. If you are sending simple chunks of data, you can use the sendall() method, as in Listing 9-5, which will handle the looping until all of the data is sent.

Listing 9-5. Using sendall() with a Socket

```
my_sock.sendall(b'Hello World')
```

For receiving data, the methods are very similar as to those for sending. One major difference is that you need to tell the methods how many bytes to read in at a time. For example, Listing 9-6 shows how you can read in the data sent above and be sure that you got all of it.

Listing 9-6. Reading Data from a Socket

```
data_in = my_sock.recv(1024)
```

This works because you know for sure that the message being sent is less than 1,024 bytes long. If the message is longer, or variable, you must loop over and over until you collect all of the separate chunks in a similar fashion to how you had to loop when you were sending data. The receiving equivalent to the sendall() method is the recv_into() method. It allows you to receive data into a preconstructed buffer, stopping either when all of the data has been received or when the buffer has been filled up. An example is given in Listing 9-7 that shows how you can read in up to 1,024 bytes into a buffer.

Listing 9-7. Receiving Data Directly into a Buffer

```
buffer = bytearray(b' ' * 1024)
my_sock.recv_into(buffer)
```

9-3. Reading an E-Mail with POP
Problem

You want to read e-mails from a POP e-mail server.

Solution

The Python standard library contains a module named poplib that encapsulates communication with a POP server.

How It Works

There are several steps involved in communicating with a POP server. The most basic initial code involves opening a connection to the POP server and authenticating, as shown in Listing 9-8.

Listing 9-8. Connecting to a POP Server and Authenticating

```
import getpass, poplib
pop_serv = poplib.POP3('192.168.0.1')
pop_serv.user(getpass.getuser())
pop_serv.pass_(getpass.getpass())
```

As you can see, you also imported the module getpass. This module helps your code securely ask for passwords from the end user. The getuser() method also queries the operating system for the end user's username. If it is the same as the username for the POP server, that's great. Otherwise, you need to either have it hardcoded within your script or you must explicitly ask the end user for their POP username. If your POP server is listening on a non-standard port, you can include it as another parameter. If the POP server you are using is more heavily secured, you need to use the POP3_SSL class instead. You can now interact with the POP server.. Listing 9-9 shows how you can get the current status of your mailbox.

Listing 9-9. Getting the Status of a POP Mailbox

```
msg_count, box_size = pop_serv.stat()
```

You can get a list of the current mailbox messages with the code in Listing 9-10.

Listing 9-10. Listing the Messages in a POP Mailbox

```
msg_list = pop_serv.list()
```

When you want to look at individual e-mails, you can use the method retr(), as in Listing 9-11.

Listing 9-11. Retrieving Individual E-Mails from a POP Server

```
message = pop_serv.retr(1)
```

This method uses the message index. (index 1 in the example) to decide which e-mail to retrieve. It also marks the selected e-mail as having been read on the POP server. You can also clean up your mailbox with the dele() method, where you hand in the e-mail index as the parameter. As with any code that interacts with system resources, don't forget to cleanly shut down any open connections with code like Listing 9-12.

Listing 9-12. Closing a POP Connection

```
pop_serv.quit()
```

9-4. Reading an E-Mail with IMAP

Problem

You need to read e-mails from an IMAP e-mail server.

Solution

The Python standard library includes a module named imaplib that simplifies communicating with an IMAP e-mail server.

How It Works

The imaplib module contains a main class that manages the communication with the IMAP server. Listing 9-13 shows how to initialize and authenticate an IMAP connection.

Listing 9-13. Creating an IMAP Connection

```
import imaplib, getpass
my_imap = imaplib.IMAP4('myimap.com')
my_imap.login(getpass.getuser(), getpass.getpass())
```

You can use the getpass module to securely get passwords from the end user. If your IMAP server uses SSL, you need to use the IMAP4_SSL class instead. IMAP provides much more organizational structure to keep your e-mails organized. Part of this includes the ability to have multiple mailboxes available. You therefore need to select a mailbox before you can work with individual e-mails. To get a list of e-mails, you need to actually do a search. Listing 9-14 shows how to get a list of all of the e-mails in your default mailbox.

Listing 9-14. Getting a List of E-Mails from IMAP

```
my_imap.select()
typ, data = my_imap.search(None, 'ALL')
```

You can then loop over the returned e-mail indices in the data variable. For each of these indices, you can then call the fetch() method. You can selectively fetch only portions of an e-mail if you desire. Listing 9-15 shows how you can get the entire e-mail from the IMAP server.

Listing 9-15. Fetching E-Mails from an IMAP Server

```
email_msg = my_imap.fetch(email_id, '(RFC822)')
```

You can then pull out those sections of an e-mail that you are interested in. IMAP has a very complete set of commands you can use to work with mailboxes and individual e-mails. For example, Listing 9-16 shows you how to delete an e-mail.

Listing 9-16. Deleting E-Mails from an IMAP Server

```
my_imap.store(email_id, '+FLAGS', '\\Deleted')
my_imap.expunge()
```

When you are all done working with your IMAP server, do not forget to clean everything up, as in Listing 9-17.

Listing 9-17. Shutting Down an IMAP Connection

```
my_imap.close()
my_imap.logout()
```

9-5. Sending an E-Mail

Problem

You need to send an e-mail.

Solution

The Python standard library includes a module named `smtplib` that can handle communication with an SMTP server.

How It Works

E-mails are sent using the SMTP protocol over the Internet. The `smtplib` includes a base class to handle connecting to the SMTP class, shown in Listing 9-18.

Listing 9-18. Connecting to an SMTP Server

```
import smtplib, getpass
my_smtp = smtplib.SMTP('my.smtp.com')
my_smtp.login(getpass.getuser(), getpass.getpass())
```

The last line is only needed if your SMTP server requires authentication. If your SMTP server uses SSL, you need to use the SMTP_SSL class instead. Once your connection is open, you can now send e-mail messages, as shown in Listing 9-19.

Listing 9-19. Sending an E-Mail Message

```
from_addr = 'me@email.com'
to_addr = 'you@email.com'
msg = 'From: me@email.com\r\nTo: you@email.com\r\n\r\nHello World'
my_smtp.sendmail(from_addr, to_addr, msg)
```

Once you have sent your e-mail, you can clean up afterwards with the `quit()` method of the SMTP object.

9-6. Reading a Web Page

Problem

You need to get the contents of a web page.

Solution

The Python standard library includes a module of classes named urllib that handles communications over several different protocols. To talk to a web server, you need to use the submodule urllib.request.

How It Works

Almost all of the complexity of making a connection to a web server is wrapped by the code within the module urllib.request. For a basic connection, you can use the method urlopen(), as in Listing 9-20.

Listing 9-20. Connecting to a Web Server

```
import urllib.request
my_web = urllib.request.urlopen('http://www.python.org')
```

You can then read the data from this URL. As with most network communications, the data gets read as a series of bytes. Listing 9-21 shows how you could read and print the first 100 bytes from the URL you are connected to.

Listing 9-21. Reading Data from a URL

```
print(my_web.read(100))
```

9-7. Posting to a Web Page

Problem

You need to communicate with a web form, either through a GET or POST.

Solution

The urllib.request module from the Python standard library supports sending form data to a web server using either the GET or POST methods.

How It Works

The urllib.request module includes a class named Request that can handle more complicated interactions with a web server. Listing 9-22 shows how to create a new connection.

Listing 9-22. Connecting to a Web Form

```
import urllib.request
mydata = b'some form data'
my_req = urllib.request.Request('http://form.host.com', data=mydata,
method='POST')
```

You can then use this new Request object in the urlopen() method, as in Listing 9-23.

Listing 9-23. Opening a Request Object

```
my_form = urllib.request.urlopen(my_req)
print(my_form.status)
print(my_form.reason)
```

9-8. Acting as a Server
Problem
You want to create a network application that listens for incoming connections.

Solution
The socket class from the Python standard library supports listening for incoming connections.

How It Works
Listing 9-24 shows how to create a socket object that will listen on a given port number.

Listing 9-24. Listening on a Network Port

```
import socket
host = ''
port = 4242
my_server = socket.socket(socket.AF_INET, socket.SOCK_STREAM)
my_server.bind((host, port))
my_server.listen(1)
```

You should be aware that you may get a warning from your firewall, depending on the settings used on your machine. After the socket has been created, you need to explicitly accept incoming connections that you can read from, as in Listing 9-25.

Listing 9-25. Accepting Incoming Connections

```
conn, addr = my_server.accept()
print('Connected from host ', addr)
data = conn.recv(1024)
```

Just as with any socket connection, don't forget to use the close() method to cleanly shut down the network connection.

CHAPTER 10

■ ■ ■

Modules and Packages

One of the biggest advantages when using Python is the large environment of available modules. There is almost literally a module for every conceivable use. In fact, this was even the topic of an XKCD web comic. In this chapter, you will look at how to tap into all of the work that has been done by installing and using the available modules. You will also look at how to package your own work into modules that you can share with others.

10-1. Importing Modules
Problem

You want to import the functionality from a given module into your current Python program.

Solution

Python includes the import keyword to handle the importation of either an entire module or only selected portions of the available functionality.

How It Works

Listing 10-1 shows a basic example of importing an entire module.

Listing 10-1. Basic Importing of a Module

```
>>> import math
```

This code imports the standard module math into the namespace of your current Python interpreter. You use the dot notation to access any of the functionality contained in this module, as in Listing 10-2.

Listing 10-2. Dot Notation for Modules

```
>>> math.sin(45)
0.8509035245341184
```

© Joey Bernard 2016
J. Bernard, *Python Recipes Handbook*, DOI 10.1007/978-1-4842-0241-8_10

To reduce the amount of typing, you can include an alias, which can be used in your program. Listing 10-3 shows how to do this for the math standard module with the as keyword.

Listing 10-3. Using Aliases

```
>>> import math as m
>>> m.cos(45)
0.5253219888177297
```

If you only need some of the functionality, you can import specific items with the from keyword, as in Listing 10-4.

Listing 10-4. Importing Parts of a Module

```
>>> from math import sin, pi
>>> sin(pi/2)
1.0
```

As you can see, this places the imported parts of the math module into the namespace of your Python program. You can then use them without using the dot notation shown previously. You can add everything from a given module with the statement in Listing 10-5.

Listing 10-5. Importing All of a Module

```
>>> from math import *
```

Note that you increase the chances of name collisions with every import. You may end up with multiple instances of a given function. The version that was last imported is the one that is used when you execute a given function name. You need to be aware of complications that may arise due to this.

10-2. Installing Modules from Source
Problem

You need to install a module from source into one of the standard library directories.

Solution

When installing from source, many modules are written to use a system called distutils, which is included with Python.

How It Works

Distutils is a very basic system that is included with Python. For simpler modules, it is more than enough to handle the installation process. The module includes a special file called setup.py that handles the details. When you install a package using distutils, you begin by unpacking the source files into a temporary directory. Then, you need to run the command given in Listing 10-6.

Listing 10-6. Installation with Distutils

```
python setup.py install
```

This will run through all of the steps required by the module in order to have it installed within one of the Python library directories.

10-3. Installing Modules from Pypi
Problem

You want to install one of the modules available within the Pypi repository.

Solution

The utility pip offers the ability to easily install modules and packages directly from the Pypi repository.

How It Works

The utility pip is not available as part of earlier versions of Python. It is available starting with versions

- Python 2 >= 2.7.9

- Python 3 >= 3.4

For earlier versions, you first need to install it. If you are using Linux, most distributions include a package for pip. For other operating systems, or if you want to install the latest version, you can download the required package from the Pypi web site (https://pip.pypa.io/en/latest/installing/) and follow the included instructions. You can then install the Python module of interest with the command in Listing 10-7.

Listing 10-7. Installing a Module with pip

```
pip install numpy
```

The really powerful part of using pip is that it will handle dependency checking. This way, you can just focus on installing the parts you need. If you are trying to install modules on a system where you don't have permissions, you can always install it in your home directory with a command like that shown in Listing 10-8.

Listing 10-8. Installing a Module in Your Home Directory

```
pip install --user numpy
```

10-4. Upgrading a Module Using pip

Problem

You need to update packages that are already installed on your system.

Solution

The pip utility includes an upgrade option that will check the Pypi repository to see if there is a newer version.

How It Works

To check for a newer version, use the command given in Listing 10-9.

Listing 10-9. Upgrading Packages

```
pip install --upgrade numpy
```

This form of the update option does an aggressive updating of all of the dependencies. Instead, you can do an "upgrade if necessary" update with the command in Listing 10-10.

Listing 10-10. Doing a Selective Upgrade

```
pip install --upgrade --no-deps numpy
pip install numpy
```

As you can see, this is actually a two-step process that should only update those dependencies that need to be updated.

CHAPTER 11

■ ■ ■

Numerics and Numpy

One of the growing areas of use for Python is within the scientific communities. One issue, which has always been an issue, is that Python is not very efficient when doing numeric calculations. Luckily, Python's very design is meant to make it relatively easy to expand its functionality. The core module that helps in scientific calculations is the Numpy module. Numpy takes the most inefficient parts of dealing with numerical calculations and outsources them to external libraries that are written in C. It uses the same standard open source libraries that are used in other applications written specifically to do heavy number-crunching.

The core of the Numpy functionality is provided by a new object called an *array*. An array is a multi-dimensional object that contains elements of one datatype. This means that the functions within the Numpy module are free to make assumptions about what can be done with the data without having to check every element as it is being accessed.

11-1. Creating Arrays
Problem
You want to create arrays to use in other Numpy functions.

Solution
The simplest way to create an array is to use the supplied creation function to take existing data within a list and convert it into a new array object. You can also use the empty function to create a new empty array object.

How It Works
The simplest form of the array function simply takes a list of values and returns a new array object, as in Listing 11-1.

Listing 11-1. Basic Array Creation

```
>>> import numpy as np
>>> list1 = [1, 2, 3.0, 4]
```

© Joey Bernard 2016
J. Bernard, *Python Recipes Handbook*, DOI 10.1007/978-1-4842-0241-8_11

```
>>> array1 = np.array(list1)
>>> array1
array([1., 2., 3., 4.])
```

This will return a one-dimensional array where each of the elements is a real number. The default behavior of the array function is to select the smallest datatype that will hold each of the elements in the original list. You can specifically select the datatype you wish to use with code such as Listing 11-2.

Listing 11-2. Creating an Array of Complex Numbers

```
>>> complex1 = np.array(list1, dtype=complex)
>>> complex1
array([1.+0.j, 2.+0.j, 3.+0.j, 4.+0.j])
```

If you have a matrix of data that you need to work with, you can simply hand in a list of lists, where each list is a row of your matrix, as in Listing 11-3.

Listing 11-3. Creating a Matrix

```
>>> matrix1 = np.array([[1, 2], [3, 4]])
>>> matrix1
array([[1, 2],
       [3, 4]])
```

If you don't have data ready, but want somewhere to store data, there is a function to create an empty array of some fixed size and of a particular datatype. For example, Listing 11-4 shows how to make an empty two-dimensional array of integers.

Listing 11-4. Creating an Empty Array of Integers

```
>>> empty1 = np.empty([2, 2], dtype=int)
>>> empty1
array([[-1073741821, -1067949133],
       [  496041986,    19249760]])
```

The issue with this function is that it may not initialize the values in any way, depending on the operating system that it is running on. You just end up with whatever data exists in those memory locations. While this is slightly faster, it does mean that you need to be aware that the initial values in your new array are junk data. If you need to start with some initial values, you can start with either zeroes or ones, as in Listing 11-5.

Listing 11-5. Creating Arrays of Zeroes and Ones

```
>>> zero1 = np.zeros((2, 3), dtype=float)
>>> zero1
array([[0., 0., 0.],
       [0., 0., 0.]])
>>> ones1 = np.ones((3, 2), dtype=int)
>>> ones1
```

```
array([[1, 1],
       [1, 1],
       [1, 1]])
```

Be aware that these two functions take a sequence of values, rather than a list, for the dimensions of the newly created array.

11-2. Copying an Array
Problem

You need to make a copy of an array for further processing.

Solution

There are three ways of sharing data across different parts of your program: no-copy access, shallow copying, and deep copying.

How It Works

You can make your arrays accessible to different parts of your program by using more than one variable at a time. In Listing 11-6, you can see how to assign the same array to two different variables.

Listing 11-6. Using No-Copy Sharing

```
>>> a = np.ones((6,), dtype=int)
>>> a
array([1, 1, 1, 1, 1, 1])
>>> b = a
```

As with the rest of Python in general, these two variables point to the same actual object in memory. You can use either to affect the actual object.

The second type of access sharing is through a shallow copy, where the data itself isn't copied, only information about the data. This is possible because an array object consists of two parts. The first is the data that is being stored within the array, while the second contains metadata about the array, such as the shape of the array. Listing 11-7 shows how to create a shallow copy by creating a view.

Listing 11-7. Shallow Copies

```
>>> view1 = ones1.view()
>>> # Do these variables point to the same object?
>>> view1 is ones1
False
>>> view1.base is ones1
True
```

83

You can access the original object by using the base property of the new view. You can change the metadata through the view, as in Listing 11-8.

Listing 11-8. Changing the Shape of a View

```
>>> view1.shape = 2,3
>>> ones1
array([[1, 1],
       [1, 1],
       [1, 1]])
>>> view1
array([[1, 1, 1],
       [1, 1, 1]])
```

This changes the shape of the matrix that the data is stored in (the number of columns and rows). The third form of copy is a deep copy, where all parts of an array are copied over. This is handled by the copy method, as in Listing 11-9.

Listing 11-9. Deep Copy of an Array

```
>>> copy1 = a.copy()
>>> a is copy1
False
>>> a is copy1.base
False
```

11-3. Accessing Array Data
Problem

You need to access individual elements or subsections of an array.

Solution

You can access individual elements with multidimensional list indexing, and subsections can be accessed with slices.

How It Works

For a one-dimensional array, you can access individual elements with the same indexing that is used for lists. Listing 11-10 shows a simple example.

Listing 11-10. Changing the Value of an Array Element

```
>>> a[1] = 2
>>> a
array([1, 2, 1, 1, 1])
```

Slices also work the same way, as in Listing 11-11.

Listing 11-11. Getting a Slice of an Array

```
>>> a[1:3]
array([2, 1])
```

One thing to note is that a slice actually returns a shallow copy of the original array, so no copy of the original data is made.

When dealing with multi-dimensional arrays, you simply need to extend the indexing by adding one extra value for each additional dimension. For example, Listing 11-12 shows how to get a single element from a matrix.

Listing 11-12. Accessing One Element from a Matrix

```
>>> ones1[1, 1] = 2
>>> ones1
array([[1, 1],
       [1, 2],
       [1, 1]])
```

If you were interested in getting a single row, you could do so with the example in Listing 11-13.

Listing 11-13. Selecting a Row from a Matrix

```
>>> ones1[1, : ]
array([1, 2])
```

11-4. Manipulating a Matrix
Problem

You need to manipulate a given matrix. This includes inversion, transposing, and calculating the norm.

Solution

Numpy includes a full suite of linear algebra tools to handle matrix manipulations.

How It Works

If you start with a simple 2-by-2 matrix, you can transpose it with the code in Listing 11-14.

Listing 11-14. Inverting a Matrix

```
>>> a = np.array([[1.0, 2.0], [3.0, 4.0]])
>>> np.linalg.inv(a)
```

```
array([[-2., 1.],
       [1.5, -0.5]])
```

The linalg submodule also provides a function to calculate the norm, as in Listing 11-15.

Listing 11-15. Finding a Norm

```
>>> np.linalg.norm(a)
5.4772255750516612
```

If you want to find the trace of a matrix, this is actually a method of the array object, as in Listing 11-16

Listing 11-16. Finding the Trace of a Matrix

```
>>> a.trace()
5.0
```

The transpose of a matrix is also a method of the array, as in Listing 11-17.

Listing 11-17. Finding the Transpose of a Matrix

```
>>> a.transpose()
array([[1., 3.],
   [2., 4.]])
```

11-5. Calculating Fast Fourier Transforms

Problem

You need to calculate a Fast Fourier Transform to look at the frequency spectrum of some collection of data.

Solution

Numpy provides a suite of different types of FFT (Fast Fourier Transform) functions.

How It Works

The discrete FFT can be used with one-dimensional, two-dimensional, or n-dimensional data. The math for each of these cases is very different, however. So Numpy provides separate functions for each of the cases, as you can see in Listing 11-18.

Listing 11-18. Discrete FFTs

```
# a is a 1-dimensional array
np.fft.fft(a)
```

```
# b is a 2-dimensional array
np.fft.fft2(b)
# c is a 3-dimensional array
np.fft.fftn(c)
```

As you can see, all of the FFT functions are actually arranged within a submodule of Numpy called fft. If you use a larger data set than appropriate for the chosen FFT function, then the last x number of axes are used. For example, if you use the array c in the one-dimensional FFT, it will use the last axis as the input for the calculation. If you wish to, you can specify a different axis with the axis parameter, as in Listing 11-19.

Listing 11-19. FFT Over Other Axes

```
np.fft.fft(c, axis=1)
```

11-6. Loading File Data into an Array
Problem

You want to load data from a file directly into an array.

Solution

Numpy can read and write plain text files, as well as its own special binary format.

How It Works

To read data from a plain text file, you can use the function loadtxt(), as in Listing 11-20.

Listing 11-20. Reading in a Text File

```
>>> txt1 = np.loadtxt('mydata.txt')
```

This function assumes that your data is laid out in columns and rows, where each line is a row. Defining the columns is done by delimiting the separate values with some other character. By default, this is done with whitespaces. The usual format with scientific data is comma-separated values (CSV). If this is the case, you can load your data with the code given in Listing 11-21.

Listing 11-21. Loading a CSV File

```
>>> txt2 = np.loadtxt('mydata.txt', delimiter=',')
```

If you have data that has been saved in Numpy's special binary format, you can use a simple load command to load it back into memory, as in Listing 11-22.

Listing 11-22. Loading Binary Data

```
>>> data = np.load('mydata.npy')
```

11-7. Saving Arrays
Problem

You have data in an array that you want to save to disk.

Solution

As with loading data, you have a few options when saving data. You can either save it to Numpy's binary format or save it to some raw text format.

How It Works

To save the data using Numpy's binary format, you can simply use the save function, as in Listing 11-23.

Listing 11-23. Saving Data Using Numpy's Binary Format

```
>>> np.save('mydata.npy', data)
```

If the filename you give it in the above call doesn't have an .npy file extension, one will be added to it. If, instead, you want to save the data to a plain text file so that it can be used by other programs, you can use the savetxt function call, as in Listing 11-24.

Listing 11-24. Saving a CSV File

```
>>> np.savetxt('mydata.csv', data, delimiter=',')
```

In this case, you explicitly set the delimiter as the comma, giving you a CSV file. If you don't set a delimiter, the default is a single space character.

11-8. Generating Random Numbers
Problem

You need to generate good quality random numbers.

Solution

Numpy provides a Mersenne Twister pseudo-random number generator, which provides very good quality random numbers. It can provide random numbers based on several distributions, like binomial, chisquare, gamma, and exponential.

How It Works

If you need random numbers using a particular distribution, you can use methods provided by RandomState to generate them. Listing 11-25 shows how to generate a random value from the geometric distribution.

Listing 11-25. Generating Random Numbers from a Geometric Distribution

```
>>> rand1 = np.random.geometric(p=0.5)
```

Most of these generators include parameters that control the details for each distribution. They usually also include a size parameter, which you can use to ask for an array of random values rather than just a single one.

If you want to have a repeatable sequence of random numbers (if you are testing code, for example), you can explicitly set a seed with the code in Listing 11-26.

Listing 11-26. Setting a Seed for Random Number Generation

```
>>> np.random.seed(42)
```

This seed also gets initialized when RandomState is created. If you don't hand one in, then RandomState will either try to read a value from the operating system random number generator (for example, /dev/urandom on Linux), or it will set the seed based on the clock.

In most cases, you can get the type of random numbers used with the code in Listing 11-27.

Listing 11-27. Generating Random Numbers

```
>>> rand2 = np.random.random()
```

11-9. Calculating Basic Statistics
Problem

You need to do basic statistics on data stored in arrays.

Solution

Numpy provides a series of statistical functions that operate on arrays of various dimensions. You can do all of the standard simple statistical analyses that you are likely to need.

How It Works

Given a set of data stored in a one-dimensional array, you can find the mean, median, variance, and standard deviation with the code in Listing 11-28.

Listing 11-28. Basic Statistics

```
>>> a = np.array([1, 2, 3, 4, 5])
>>> np.mean(a)
3.0
>>> np.median(a)
3.0
>>> np.var(a)
2.0
>>> np.std(a)
1.4142135623730951
```

If you have multi-dimensional data, you can select which axis to calculate these statistics along.

11-10. Computing Histograms
Problem

You have a series of data that you need to group into bins and calculate a histogram.

Solution

Numpy contains a handful of related functions to work with histograms, both one-dimensional and multi-dimensional.

How It Works

Assuming you have your data series stored in the variable b, you can generate a histogram with the code in Listing 11-29.

Listing 11-29. Generating a Simple Histogram

```
>>> b = np.array([1,2,1,2,3,1,2,3,3,2,1])
>>> np.histogram(b)
(array([4, 0, 0, 0, 0, 4, 0, 0, 0, 3], dtype=int64),
 array([ 1. ,  1.2,  1.4,  1.6,  1.8,  2. ,  2.2,  2.4,  2.6,  2.8,  3. ]))
```

By default, Numpy will try to group your data into 10 bins. The first array tells you how many values are in each bin and the second array tells you the boundaries of each bin. You can set the number of bins by adding in a second parameter, as in Listing 11-30.

Listing 11-30. Histograms with a Set Bin Count

```
>>> np.histogram(b, 3)
(array([4, 4, 3], dtype=int64),
 array([ 1. ,  1.66666667,  2.33333333,  3. ]))
```

CHAPTER 12

Concurrency

Computers have been getting faster and faster over the decades, but we are starting to bump into some of the limitations of physics. This means that in order to get more work done, we need to move to using multiple processes in parallel. There are several techniques available within Python to support concurrent execution of code.

The first technique is to use threads to break up the work. The main problem with this method is that it suffers from the bottleneck caused by the GIL (Global Interpreter Lock). Threads that are doing I/O or using certain modules, such as numpy, can get around this bottleneck. If you need to do more computational work, you may want to uses processes instead. In this chapter, you will look at several of the available options within Python.

12-1. Creating a Thread

Problem

You want to create a thread to do some task.

Solution

The Python standard library contains a module named threading that contains a Thread class.

How It Works

The main class, Thread, provides for running multiple functions in parallel. Listing 12-1 shows how to create and run a basic thread.

Listing 12-1. Creating a Thread

```
import threading
def print_sum():
    print('The sum of 1 and 2 is 3')
my_thread = threading.Thread(target=print_sum)
my_thread.start()
```

You should note that the thread that you created won't start executing the target function until you call the start() method. If the function is a longer-running one, you can check to see whether it is still running by using the is_alive() method. It will return a Boolean value telling you whether it is still running or not. If you can't continue without the results from a given thread, you can call the join() method to force a wait until the thread is all done.

12-2. Using Locks
Problem
You need to control thread access to a particular resource.

Solution
The threading module includes a Lock class to control thread access.

How It Works
Locks are used when threads need to access global resources safely. Listing 12-2 shows how to create and use a lock object.

Listing 12-2. Creating a Lock Object

```
import threading
sum = 0
my_lock = threading.Lock()
def adder():
    global sum, my_lock
    my_lock.acquire()
    sum = sum + 1
    my_lock.release()
my_thread = threading.thread(target=adder)
my_thread.start()
```

By default, the acquire() method of the lock object blocks if the lock was already acquired by another thread. If, instead, you want to be able to do something else while waiting for a lock, you can use the parameter blocking=False in the acquire() method. It will return right away, giving you a Boolean value as to whether the acquire attempt succeeded or not.

12-3. Setting a Barrier
Problem
You need to synchronize thread activity by setting a common stop point.

Solution

The threading module includes a barrier object that can be used to set a common stopping point.

How It Works

In many languages, using a barrier involves a simple function call, whereas in Python, barriers are managed with an object. Listing 12-3 shows how you can create a barrier for five threads.

Listing 12-3. Creating a Barrier Object

```
import threading
b = threading.Barrier(5, timeout=10)
```

As you can see, you have to explicitly tell the barrier object how many threads will be using it. You can also set a timeout for the maximum amount of time that the threads are allowed to wait for the barrier to be satisfied. To actually use the barrier object, each thread needs to call the wait() method.

12-4. Creating a Process
Problem

You need to create multiple processes for multiprocessing.

Solution

The Python standard library includes a module named multiprocessing that contains a Process class.

How It Works

If your code is being affected by the GIL, one way around it is by using the class Process to spawn other tasks outside the main Python process. The interface is very similar to that for threads. For example, Listing 12-4 shows how to create a new process and start it running.

Listing 12-4. Creating a New Process

```
import multiprocessing
def adder(a, b):
    return a+b
proc1 = multiprocessing.Process(target=adder, args=(2,2))
proc1.start()
proc1.join()
```

As you can see, your newly created process object is executed with the start() method, and you can force the main part of your code to wait for results with the join() method.

12-5. Communicating Between Processes
Problem

You need to send information from one process object to another.

Solution

The multiprocessing module has two classes that can be used for inter-process communications: the pipe and queue classes.

How It Works

Because process objects execute outside the main part of the Python interpreter, communicating with them, or between them, requires a bit more work. The most basic form of communication is the pipe. Listing 12-5 shows how to create a new pipe object.

Listing 12-5. Creating a Pipe

```
import multiprocessing
def func(pipe_end):
    pipe_end.send(['hello', 'world'])
    pipe_end.close()
parent_end, child_end = multiprocessing.Pipe()
proc1 = multiprocessing.Process(target=func, args=(child_end,))
proc1.start()
print(parent_end.recv())
proc1.join()
```

As you can see, pipes are a simple communication channel with two ends that processes can read to and write from. Pipes are full-duplex, so messages can be sent from both ends. The major problem with pipes, however, is that the ends can only be used by one process at a time. If two processes try to read from or write to the same end at the same time, the data could be corrupted.

A different technique is to use a queue object to communicate with. A queue is a FIFO (First In, First Out) object. It can accept data from multiple processes and multiple processes can pull data off the queue. Listing 12-6 show how you can create and use a queue object.

Listing 12-6. Creating a Queue

```
import multiprocessing
def func(queue1):
    queue1.put(['hello', 'world'])
```

```
my_queue = multiprocessing.Queue()
proc1 = multiprocessing.Process(target=func, args=(my_queue,))
proc1.start()
print(my_queue.get())
proc1.join()
```

12-6. Creating a Pool of Workers
Problem

You need to start up and run a pool of processes.

Solution

The Python standard library module, multiprocessing, contains a Pool class to manage a task queue.

How It Works

When you have a whole series of tasks that need to be handled, you can create a pool of processes to work through those tasks. Listing 12-7 shows how to create a pool of four worker processes and have them work on a stack of tasks.

Listing 12-7. Creating a Pool of Processes

```
import multiprocessing
def adder(a):
    return a+a
pool1 = multiprocessing.Pool(processes=4)
```

This newly created pool object has several different methods to divide the tasks among the processes. There are both blocking and non-blocking versions of these methods. For example, Listing 12-8 shows how to use the map method.

Listing 12-8. Mapping a Function to a Pool of Processes

```
# This method blocks untill all processes return
pool1.map(adder, range(10))
# This method returns a result object
results = pool1.map_async(adder, range(10))
results.wait()
```

The last line in Listing 12-8 is used to block and wait until all of the results are returned. You can use it when you are ready to use all of the results from the farmed out tasks.

12-7. Creating a Subprocess

Problem

You need to spawn a subprocess to handle an external task.

Solution

The Python standard library contains a module named subprocess that can spawn external processes.

How It Works

The subprocess module is intended to replace the older os.system and os.spawn methods for running external processes. The module contains a method named run() that is the usual method for using subprocesses. For example, Listing 12-9 shows how you can get a list of the files in the current directory on either a Linux box or a Mac OS machine.

Listing 12-9. Spawning a Subprocess

```
import subprocess
results = subprocess.run(['ls', '-l'], stdout=subprocess.PIPE)
print(results.stdout)
```

The returned results object contains a lot of information about how the external process ran, including the exit code.

12-8. Scheduling Events

Problem

You need to schedule tasks for some later time.

Solution

The Python standard library contains a module named sched that has several objects and methods that are useful in scheduling work at different times.

How It Works

To schedule future tasks, you can create a Scheduler object to can take a queue of events and manage them. You can use the enter() method to add events to the queue, as in Listing 12-10.

Listing 12-10. Creating a Scheduler

```python
import sched, time
def print_time():
    print(time.time())
my_sched = sched.scheduler()
my_sched.enter(10, 1, print_time)
```

The enter() method takes a delay, a priority, and a function to execute when the event triggers. If you want to have an event trigger at a specific time instead, you can use the enterabs() method. Once you have a larger list of events, you can always check the current queue with the scheduler's queue attribute. If you get to the end of your program, you can force your code to stop and wait until all the events have finished with the run() method.

CHAPTER 13

Utilities

All programming languages use external utility programs to make development and execution easier on the programmer. Python is no different in this regard. In this chapter, you will take a look at some of the most common external utilities that are used when writing code for the Python programming language. These include utilities to set up environments, better interpreters, an entire coding environment, and even a shell replacement.

13-1. Creating a Virtual Environment
Problem

You want to create and use a virtual environment for a particular Python program.

Solution

The usual way to create and manage virtual environments is through the virtualenv utility.

How It Works

One of the strengths of Python, its very healthy selection of third-party modules, is also one of its problems. You can very quickly end up with a massive library of modules that are only used some of the time. One way of minimizing this issue is to set up a separate environment for each project so that you only have the modules you require for said project installed within this environment. The first step is to install virtualenv. Listing 13-1 shows how to do this with pip.

Listing 13-1. Installing virtualenv

```
pip install virtualenv
```

Once it is installed, you can create new virtual environments. Listing 13-2 show how you can create a new, blank, environment for a new project.

Listing 13-2. Creating a New Virtual Environment

```
virtualenv project1
```

This command creates a new directory named `project1` and installs everything you need to run Python programs, as well as install and manage modules. In order to use this new environment, you change the directory to the `project1` subdirectory and source the shell script `./bin/activate`. There are versions for many of the most used Linux shells, as well as the Windows `cmd` shell and the Windows `powershell`. This script sets several environment variables to use the included interpreter and module library.

When you are done using the environment in question, you can run the script `deactivate` to undo the environmental changes. If you decide that you no longer need a particular virtual environment, you can simply delete the entire related directory and all of its contents. The full documentation is available at `https://virtualenv.pypa.io/en/stable/`.

13-2. Using the Ipython Shell

Problem

You want to use a better interpreter shell, rather than the default one used by the Python interpreter.

Solution

The IPython interpreter shell provides many enhancements over the default Python interpreter shell.

How It Works

You can install the latest version of IPython with the command shown in Listing 13-3.

Listing 13-3. Installing IPython

```
pip install ipython
```

To use the interpreter, you simply need to execute the command `ipython` from a command prompt. It is very similar to many Linux shells in that it provides functions like tab completion, command history, and more sophisticated command editing.

One of the more powerful functions within the IPython interpreter is the set of commands called magics. These special commands begin with a % sign, followed by some keyword. For example, Listing 13-4 shows how you can time a given operation.

Listing 13-4. Using the timeit Magic Function

```
%timeit x = range(1000000)
```

There are magics that can run external scripts, load or save commands, and even affect the color of the IPython interpreter. Listing 13-5 shows how to save a series of previous commands to a file.

Listing 13-5. Saving to a File with Ipython Magics

```
# Saving a series of commands to a file
%save myfile.py 2-5 10
```

This way, you can save the useful lines from a session of experimentation. The load magic function reads in the contents of a file into the IPython front end, as if you had just typed them in. Listing 13-6 shows what happens if you load a file that has a single print statement.

Listing 13-6. Loading a File with IPython Magic

```
In [7]: %load myfile.py

In [8]: print("Hello world")
```

You can also create your own magic functions that can further extend the functionality of IPython. The main documentation can be found at http://ipython. readthedocs.io/en/stable/index.html.

13-3. Using the Jupyter Environment
Problem

You want to use a more complete environment for ease of interactive development.

Solution

You can use Jupyter, which is a fork of the web interface to IPython. It provides an interface similar to commercial applications such as Maple, Mathematica, or Matlab.

How It Works

The first step is to install Jupyter on your system. Listing 13-7 shows how you can do this with pip.

Listing 13-7. Installing Jupyter

```
pip install jupyter
```

From a command prompt, executing the command jupyter notebook will start up a web server and Python engine, and then start up a web browser that connects to the newly started server. Jupyter is quickly becoming the de facto platform for doing science with Python. Along with the enhanced functionality inherited from IPython, Jupyter also includes functionality such as the ability to draw inline matplotlib graphs. There is actually a very complete set of other utilities as part of Jupyter, such as a notebook viewer and a notebook grading utility for when you are using Jupyter within a classroom environment. The main documentation is located at http://jupyter.readthedocs.io/en/latest/index.html.

13-4. Using xonsh as a Replacement Shell

Problem

The command shell on Linux or Mac OS is a very personal choice. It is the environment you use to interact with everything on your machine. You may want to use Python as the command shell for working on a computer.

Solution

You can use a new project called xonsh as a replacement command shell.

How It Works

Installation of xonsh can be done with pip, as in Listing 13-8.

Listing 13-8. Installing xonsh

```
pip install xonsh
```

Once it is installed, xonsh can be used like any other command shell. xonsh is at least partly bash-compatible. This refers to the ability to run other programs, have and use a command history, and handle background jobs. Along with this usual functionality, you also have all of the power of a Python engine underlying all of it. This means that you can use Python modules to add functionality within your command shell. Listing 13-9 shows how you can get random numbers directly from the command line.

Listing 13-9. Using Python Modules within xonsh

```
jbernard@DESKTOP-QPKN2QC ~ <branch-timeout> $ import numpy as np
jbernard@DESKTOP-QPKN2QC ~ <branch-timeout> $ np.random.random()
0.48053753953641054
```

The main documentation site is located at http://xon.sh/index.html.

CHAPTER 14

Testing and Debugging

This book has focused on giving you tips and tricks on how to write Python code. Very little space has been spent on making this code as good as it could be. In this chapter, you will look at techniques to analyze your code's performance. You will also look at ways to debug your program when errors and mistakes creep into the code you are writing.

14-1. Timing a Section of Code
Problem

You want to time a section of code to see how long it takes to run.

Solution

The Python standard library includes a package named timeit that can run code multiple times and get average runtimes.

How It Works

If you have Python statements, you can run them through the timeit package from the command line, as in Listing 14-1.

Listing 14-1. Using the timeit Command

```
python -m timeit 'print(42)'

10000000 loops, best of 3: 0.035 usec per loop
```

Listing 14-2 shows how you do a similar task from within the Python interpreter.

© Joey Bernard 2016
J. Bernard, *Python Recipes Handbook*, DOI 10.1007/978-1-4842-0241-8_14

Listing 14-2. Timing Python Code with timeit

```
>>> import timeit
>>> timeit.timeit('42*42', number=1000)
0.0001980264466965309
```

As you can see, you need to explicitly tell timeit how many times to run your Python statements.

14-2. Profiling Code
Problem

You want to profile your code to see where performance bottlenecks are located.

Solution

The Python standard library includes two packages that can be used to profile your code: profile and cProfile.

How It Works

Both profile and cProfile provide a common interface with profiling tools to look at your code's performance. The major difference between the two packages is their own performance when profiling your code. The package cProfile is written in C, so it only minimally impacts the runtime of your own code. To get this speed, however, it needs to be compiled for whichever systems you are profiling your code on. The package profile is written in pure Python, so it will run more slowly than cProfile. The advantages, however, are that profile will run anywhere your code will run, and it is easy to extend the functionality of profile to add in extra features.

There are several ways to use the profiling packages with your own code. If your code is already bundled within a set of functions, you can simply run it under the profiler, as in Listing 14-3.

Listing 14-3. Running the Profiler

```
>>> def my_func():
...     return 42

>>> import profile
>>> profile.run('my_func')
         4 function calls in 0.000 seconds

   Ordered by: standard name

   ncalls  tottime  percall  cumtime  percall filename:lineno(function)
```

```
1    0.000    0.000    0.000    0.000 :0(exec)
1    0.000    0.000    0.000    0.000 :0(setprofile)
1    0.000    0.000    0.000    0.000 <string>:1(<module>)
1    0.000    0.000    0.000    0.000 profile:0(my_func)
0    0.000             0.000          profile:0(profiler)
```

As you can see, you get quite a bit of information on how much time is being spent in each of the function calls within your code. There are several other methods of running your own code through the profiler. If the program you want to profile is already packaged as a script file, you can choose instead to run it through the profiler from the command line, as in Listing 14-4.

Listing 14-4. Running the Profiler from the Command Line

```
python -m profile -o myscript.out myscript.py
```

This command will dump a binary version of the profiling results into the file myscript.out. This is handy if you need to run the profiling step on a remote machine but want to look at the results at a later time. You can see the results by using the pstats package. Listing 14-5 shows how you can get basic statistics from this binary file.

Listing 14-5. Reading a Profiling Run

```
>>> import pstats
>>> p = pstats.Stats('myscript.out')
>>> p.print_stats()
Sun Sep 11 20:39:14 2016    myscript.out

        9 function calls in 0.000 seconds

   Random listing order was used

   ncalls  tottime  percall  cumtime  percall filename:lineno(function)
        2    0.000    0.000    0.000    0.000 C:\Users\berna_000\
Anaconda3_4\lib\encodings\cp850.py:18(encode)
        1    0.000    0.000    0.000    0.000 :0(print)
        2    0.000    0.000    0.000    0.000 :0(charmap_encode)
        1    0.000    0.000    0.000    0.000 :0(setprofile)
        1    0.000    0.000    0.000    0.000 myscript.py:1(<module>)
        1    0.000    0.000    0.000    0.000 profile:0(<code object
<module> at 0x000001F1B82040C0, file "myscript.py", line 1>)
        0    0.000             0.000          profile:0(profiler)
        1    0.000    0.000    0.000    0.000 :0(exec)


<pstats.Stats object at 0x000001F1B8208550>
```

There are lots of options within pstats to help you dig into the resulting output file.

14-3. Tracing Subroutines

Problem

You need to trace what subroutines your code uses to see what other functions are being used by your program.

Solution

The Python standard library includes a package named trace that can give you coverage listings, caller/callee relationships, and listings of all called functions.

How It Works

The trace module can be used from the command line, which is useful if you already have your code bundled within a script file. Listing 14-6 shows how you can do this to do a trace of your script.

Listing 14-6. Tracing a Program

```
python -m trace --trace myscript.py

--- modulename: myscript, funcname: <module>
myscript.py(1): print('42')
 --- modulename: cp850, funcname: encode
cp850.py(19):            return codecs.charmap_encode(input,self.
errors,encoding_map)[0]
42 --- modulename: cp850, funcname: encode
cp850.py(19):            return codecs.charmap_encode(input,self.
errors,encoding_map)[0]

 --- modulename: trace, funcname: _unsettrace
trace.py(77):           sys.settrace(None)
```

You can use the following trace options to collect different kinds of data:

--count	Count how many times each statement is executed
--trace	Display lines as they are executed
--listfuncs	Display functions as they are executed
--trackcalls	Display the calling relationships

You can also use trace from within your Python code. It includes two main classes: Trace and CoverageResults. Listing 14-7 shows how you can trace through a single command.

Listing 14-7. Tracing a Command in Python Code

```
>>> import trace
>>> tracer = trace.Trace()
>>> tracer.run('print("Hello World")')
Hello World
 --- modulename: trace, funcname: _unsettrace
trace.py(80):           sys.settrace(None)
```

14-4. Tracing Memory Allocations
Problem

You need to trace memory allocations within your program to see how memory is being used.

Solution

The Python standard library includes a module named tracemalloc that can trace through memory allocations and statistics on memory usage.

How It Works

To use tracemalloc, you need to start it up so that it can collect memory information over time. Listing 14-8 shows how you can get the top 10 offenders in memory usage.

Listing 14-8. Getting Memory Statistics

```
import tracemalloc
tracemalloc.start()
# Run you code here
snapshot = tracemalloc.take_snapshot()
top_stats = snapshot.statistics('lineno')
for curr_stat in top_stats:
    print(curr_stat)
```

You can also look at how memory usage changes over time by taking multiple snapshots. Helpfully, the snapshot objects have a method called compare_to() that allows you to see how they differ, as shown in Listing 14-9.

Listing 14-9. Comparing Two Memory Snapshots

```
import tracemalloc
tracemalloc.start()
snapshot1 = tracemalloc.take_snapshot()
# run your code
```

```
snapshot2 = tracemalloc.take_snapshot()
top_stats = snapshot2.compare_to(snapshot1, 'lineno')
```

You can then look at the top_stats object to see how memory usage changed over time.

14-5. Performing Unit Tests
Problem
You want to run unit tests on your code to verify program behavior.

Solution
The Python standard library includes a module named unittest that can be used to build test cases for your code.

How It Works
To create unit tests, you need to subclass the TestCase class and add in the test cases that will verify your code. Each test case has to be named with *test* as the prefix. You then use assertEqual(), assertTrue(), assertFalse(), and assertRaises() to verify conditions. A simple example is shown in Listing 14-10.

Listing 14-10. A Simple Test Case

```
import unittest
class MyTestCase(unittest.TestCase):
    def test_the_answer(self):
        assertEqual(self.curr_val, 42)

if __name__ == '__main__':
    unittest.main()
```

This is just a short introduction to using test cases within Python. There are entire books devoted to organizing and designing test driven code.

14-6. Debugging Code
Problem
You need to debug problems that have crept into your code.

Solution
The Python standard library includes a package named pdb that provides a debugging interface into the operation of your code.

How It Works

If you want to use it interactively, you can import the pdb module within your Python interpreter and use it to run your code, as shown in Listing 14-11.

Listing 14-11. Running Code Under the Debugger

```
>>> import pdb
>>> pdb.run('my_func()')
```

This enters the interactive mode of the debugger. This is highlighted by the prompt (pdb). The interface is similar to other text-based debuggers, such as gdb. If you want to run an entire script in the debugger, you do this from the command line, as in Listing 14-12.

Listing 14-12. Debugging a Script File

```
python -m pdb myscript.py
```

This will drop you into the post-mortem session of the debugger if your script exits abnormally. If you know roughly where the issue might be located, you can add a line to break into the debugger, as in Listing 14-13.

Listing 14-13. Dropping into the Debugger

```
import pdb; pdb.set_trace()
```

You can then step through your code to locate the source of the problems in your code. If you are in an interactive session, you can run your code through the debugger manually. Listing 14-14 shows a sample of stepping through a function.

Listing 14-14. Stepping Through a Function with pdb

```
>>> import pdb
>>> def myfunc():
....    print("Hello World")

>>> pdb.run('myfunc()')
> <string>(1)<module>()->None
(Pdb) step
--Call--
> <ipython-input-11-b0e3e2c712c8>(1)myfunc()
-> def myfunc():
(Pdb) step
> <ipython-input-11-b0e3e2c712c8>(2)myfunc()
-> print("Hello World")
(Pdb) step
Hello World
--Return--
> <ipython-input-11-b0e3e2c712c8>(2)myfunc()->None
```

```
-> print("Hello World")
(Pdb) step
--Return--
> <string>(1)<module>()->None
(Pdb) step
> /usr/lib/python3.4/bdb.py(435)run()
-> self.quitting = True
(Pdb) step
```

CHAPTER 15

■ ■ ■

C and Other Extensions

One of the great things about Python is that it is not the best tool for every job, and more importantly, it knows that it isn't the best tool for every job. Because of this self-awareness, Python was designed from the beginning to be extensible with code written in C. This capability is provided by a module called Cython, which is available from http://cython. org. In this chapter, you will look at some of the different ways you can include Cython within your own Python programs in order to improve its performance or add extra functionality.

15-1. Compiling Python Code

Problem

You want to compile your Python code to C to get a speedup.

Solution

The Cython package provides a mechanism for mixing compiled C code with Python.

How It Works

The initial setup applies to all of the following examples within this chapter. You need to have a C compiler on your system. If you are running Linux or Mac OS, then you can use gcc as the required compiler. To get the compiler on Mac OS, you need to install the XCode package. As for Windows, there are more steps involved. There is an entire appendix within the Cython documentation just for instructions on how to set up Windows. As well, you will need Cython installed. You can either install it from source, or you can install it using pip, as in Listing 15-1.

Listing 15-1. Installing Cython with pip

```
pip install --user cython
```

Once everything is installed, you need to write the Python code that is to be compiled into C. This code is saved in a file ending with .pyx, rather than .py. This Cython source file is then compiled in one of several different ways. For larger projects, the most flexible and robust way to handle the compilation is to write a setup.py file and use distutils. This method is a bit too complex to introduce in such a short space. Happily, there are a couple of other simpler methods to start using Cython with your code right away.

Listing 15-2 shows a sample .pyx file that just has a single function in it.

Listing 15-2. HelloWorld.pyx File

```
def print_msg():
    print("Hello World")
```

Cython includes a module named pyximport, which will compile .pyx files in the background when you try to import them. Listing 15-3 shows how you can use this within an interactive Python session.

Listing 15-3. Using pyximport

```
>>> import pyximport
>>> pyximport.install()
>>> import HelloWorld
>>> print_msg()
Hello World
```

This works fine for entire source files. If the section of code you wish to compile is even shorter, you can have Cython compile it inline, directly in the middle of your Python source code. Listing 15-4 gives one example of inlining compiled code.

Listing 15-4. Using Inlined Cython Code

```
>>> import cython
>>> def my_adder(a, b):
...     ret = cython.inline("return a+b")
...
```

The compiled version of the inline code is cached in order to improve efficiency.

15-2. Using Static Types
Problem

You want to speed up access to objects by giving them a type.

Solution

You can install the Cython module, along with a supported C compiler, to define new types that are accessed and worked with much faster than with Python objects.

How It Works

To use static typing, Cython introduces a new keyword called cdef. When this is used, you can get even more speedups than you achieved by compiling your Python code with Cython. Listing 15-5 shows an example of an integration problem.

Listing 15-5. Pure Python Integration Problem

```
def f(x):
    return x**2-42

def integrate_f(a, b, N):
    s = 0
    dx = (b-a)/N
    for I in range(N):
        s += f(a+i*dx)
    return s*dx
```

Compiling this under Cython will provide a certain amount of speedup, but there is still type checking that happens. This is especially costly on loops, where variables are accessed many times. Listing 15-6 shows the same example, except using the cdef keyword.

Listing 15-6. Integration Problem Using Static Typing

```
def f(double x):
    return x**2-42

def integrate_f(double a, double b, int N):
    cdef int i
    cdef double s, dx
    s = 0
    dx = (b-a)/N
    for I in range(N):
        s += f(a+i*dx)
    return s*dx
```

This code removes all of those costly type checks and can be a great boon when trying to optimize your code. In order to compile these files, you can use the Cython command line utility to generate a C source file that can be compiled to a shared object to be imported within Python. Assuming the above examples were saved in a file named mycode.pyx, Listing 15-7 shows how to use GCC.

Listing 15-7. Compiling Cython Code Manually

```
cython myfile.pyx
gcc -shared -o myfile.so myfile.c `python3-config --includes`
```

You can then import this newly compiled shared object from within Python.

15-3. Calling Python from C

Problem

You want to be able to call Python code from within a C program.

Solution

The standard library includes the header file called Python.h, which makes Python callable from C.

How It Works

There are two main functions that are available when you want to call Python code from C: Py_Initialize() and Py_Finalize(). The first function starts the Python interpreter and the second function shuts it down again. Between the two function calls, you can run your Python code. Listing 15-8 shows an example where you can execute a string of Python code.

Listing 15-8. Running Python Code from C

```
#include "Python.h"
void run_pycode(const char* code) {
    Py_Initialize();
    PyRun_SimpleString(code);
    Py_Finalize();
}
```

This works fine for shorter pieces of code, but if you have an entire script, you can run it from your C program, as shown in Listing 15-9.

Listing 15-9. Running a Python Script from C

```
#include "Python.h"
Int main() {
    Py_Initialize();
    FILE* file = fopen("./my_script.py", "r");
    PyRun_SimpleFile(file, "./my_script.py");
    Py_Finalize();
}
```

15-4. Calling C from Python

Problem

You want to call external C code from a Python program.

Solution

The standard Python API includes code to help connect Python and C. The Cython package makes this communication easier.

How It Works

The keywords cdef extern from tell Cython a location from which to import C functions. Listing 15-10 shows an example of a .pyx file.

Listing 15-10. Importing External C Code

```
cdef extern from "hello_world.c":
    void print_msg()
```

Listing 15-11 shows the related C source code file.

Listing 15-11. Imported C Code

```
static void print_msg() {
    printf("Hello World");
}
```

This is a much simpler interface for importing C code than the standard API included in Python.

CHAPTER 16

■ ■ ■

Arduino and RPi Recipes

For amateur inventors, the Raspberry PI and the Arduino are a huge resource for designing and building one's own technology. The Raspberry Pi has become the de facto single board computer (or SBC), and Python has become the de facto language used on the Pi. In other cases, you may actually need a microcontroller to provide either an interface to a computer or to act as a more limited control unit. In these cases, the Arduino, in all its variations, has become the standard. While you will only explore the Arduino and the Raspberry Pi in this chapter, there are several other options available that you may want to check out.

16-1. Sending Data to an Arduino

Problem

You want to send data or instructions to an Arduino.

Solution

You can use the Python module `pyserial` to communicate with the Arduino over a serial connection.

How It Works

You can install `pyserial` with `pip`, as shown in Listing 16-1.

Listing 16-1. Installing pyserial

```
pip install --user pyserial
```

You need to have a program preloaded on your Arduino that is expecting to accept instructions or data. Once this is done, use a serial cable to connect your Arduino to a computer that is running Python. You can then have your Python code send information to the Arduino with code such as that in Listing 16-2.

© Joey Bernard 2016
J. Bernard, *Python Recipes Handbook*, DOI 10.1007/978-1-4842-0241-8_16

Listing 16-2. Sending Data to an Arduino

```
>>> import serial
>>> ser = serial.Serial('/dev/tty.usbserial', 9600)
>>> ser.write(b'5')
```

In the second line, you need to replace the device entry, /dev/tty.usbserial, with whatever location is appropriate for your system. In the write() method, the preceding b is needed to convert the Unicode string to a simple byte string.

16-2. Reading Data from an Arduino
Problem

You want to read data from an Arduino.

Solution

Again, you can use the pyserial module to read data from the serial connection with the Arduino.

How It Works

Assuming that the code that is preloaded on your Arduino is expecting to send data out over the serial connection, you can use the Python module pyserial to read this data. An example is given by Listing 16-3.

Listing 16-3. Reading Data from an Arduino

```
>>> import serial
>>> ser = serial.Serial('/dev/tty.usbserial', 9600)
>>> data = ser.readline()
```

The readline() method expects a newline at the end of the data being sent, so be sure your Arduino code sends that along with each output of data.

16-3. Writing to the Raspberry Pi's GPIO Bus
Problem

You want to write output on the Raspberry Pi's GPIO bus.

Solution

The RPi.GPIO module provides an interface between your Python code and the physical GPIO bus.

How It Works

The RPi.GPIO module is included in the package repository for Raspbian. Listing 16-4 shows how to install it on your Raspberry Pi.

Listing 16-4. Installing the RPi.GPIO Module

```
sudo apt-get install python-dev python-rpi.gpio
```

In order to use the RPi.GPIO module, there are several steps involved to set up the GPIO bus and handle the communication. Listing 16-5 shows an example of setting a GPIO pin to high.

Listing 16-5. Setting a GPIO Pin to High

```
import RPi.GPIO as GPIO
GPIO.setmode(GPIO.BOARD)
GPIO.setup(1, GPIO.OUT, initial=GPIO.LOW)
GPIO.output(1, GPIO.HIGH)
```

The setmode() method sets up the pin numbering scheme to use. GPIO.BOARD uses the pin numbering that is on the board itself. The setup() method sets up a particular pin as either input or output, and optionally sets the initial value of the pin. You can then send output to the pin in question with the output() method. As you can see, the GPIO bus outputs binary data, as either a low or a high.

16-4. Reading from the Raspberry Pi's GPIO Bus

Problem

You want to read input from the Raspberry Pi's GPIO bus.

Solution

You can use the RPi.GPIO Python module to read data in from the GPIO bus.

How It Works

Listing 16-6 provides a basic example of how to read in data from one of the GPIO pins.

Listing 16-6. Reading Data from the GPIO Bus

```
import RPi.GPIO as GPIO
GPIO.setup(1, GPIO.IN)
if GPIO.input(1):
    print('Input was HIGH')
else:
    print('Input was LOW')
```

As you can see, the inputs are received as either binary highs or lows.

Index

© Joey Bernard 2016
J. Bernard, *Python Recipes Handbook*, DOI 10.1007/978-1-4842-0241-8

Get the eBook for only $4.99!

Why limit yourself?

Now you can take the weightless companion with you wherever you go and access your content on your PC, phone, tablet, or reader.

Since you've purchased this print book, we are happy to offer you the eBook for just $4.99.

Convenient and fully searchable, the PDF version enables you to easily find and copy code—or perform examples by quickly toggling between instructions and applications.

To learn more, go to http://www.apress.com/us/shop/companion or contact support@apress.com.

Printed in the United States
By Bookmasters